The Group
Approach to Shakespeare

A
MIDSUMMER
NIGHT'S
DREAM

The Group Approach to Shakespeare

ROMEO AND JULIET
THE MERCHANT OF VENICE
TWELFTH NIGHT
A MIDSUMMER NIGHT'S DREAM

The Group
Approach to Shakespeare

A
MIDSUMMER
NIGHT'S
DREAM

David Adland

LONGMAN

LONGMAN GROUP LIMITED
London

Associated companies, branches and representatives
throughout the world

© *This edition Longman Group Ltd 1973*

First published 1973

ISBN 0 582 20087 3

PRINTED IN GREAT BRITAIN BY
LOWE & BRYDONE (PRINTERS) LIMITED

CONTENTS

———— • ————

INTRODUCTION

The easiest and perhaps the most appropriate way of introducing this book is to repeat, 'The play's the thing...'. It may be read, it may be studied in depth, it may be littered with notes and cross-references, it may be analysed line by line and freely quoted in essays and examinations; and it may be acted.

Acting usually means the preparation for a school production of the whole play, or of selected scenes, learnt, rehearsed and performed as part of some specific entertainment. Sometimes, too, students may be taken to see a professional performance of the play and then develop a variety of individual and group projects from their visit and from their study of the play.

This book aims to bring the acting experience into the class-room or the drama hall, to engage all the students in the activity, and to assist, through private performance, the student's understanding of the lines or the scene he is then studying. This book provides practical material for every scene in the play; in this play most of the scenes are divided into two or, more often, three sections for particular work. It is not necessary to work through the book scene by scene or to complete all the suggested activities. The teacher, as always, can select and direct what work should be attempted, as well as simply using the material as a starting point for his students' own interests.

Time is always a vital factor in the classroom and for this reason much of the work can be quickly prepared by pairs of players and performed in a few minutes. For example, each scene or section of a scene begins with *Conversations for two*, which offer suggestions for imaginative or factual talking without moving from the desk. They can be played by pairs of boys or pairs of girls, or mixed pairs, and the text notes where the male or female roles can be reversed. A reading of these Conversations, the selection of which one to do, a check on the original text, and a rehearsal of the actual conversation should take no more than ten minutes; a final version, whether public or private, two or three minutes.

Although Conversations can be played without movement and be presented to the rest of the class from where the players are seated or from the front of the class, they can be acted in the usual way if there is sufficient space. Apart from anything else, movement (and only two players are involved) will give added liveliness and emphasis to the dialogue and a focus for the attention of the class. Where there is more space, and when time is available, the Conversation can be developed into more detailed situations using a larger cast.

A number of Shakespeare's dramatic methods are briefly described and illustrated and work is suggested. These include the soliloquy, the supernatural, the play within the play, climax, the incident described, visual comedy and verbal drama. These are large and important aspects of the play, which can be illuminated by performance and be the basis of interesting and valuable research which may be presented as a sequence of extracts with linking material and commentary from a narrator. Other projects which can be written, discussed or performed are suggested in *Imaginative written work* at the end of each Act.

Some techniques make only an occasional appearance in the text, being used as the best means of exploring a particular point at a particular moment. The teacher will see that some of these can be used equally well on other occasions which he can point out to his students. In Act IV there is *Group Interview* in which the characters themselves look into one another's characters and motives; then *Objectives* shows how these motives, in the form of key words, can be used in expressing the characters' feelings in modern speech. Later, the whole of Act IV is organized into practical work for groups using the technique of freezing the action into a frame which makes a significant dramatic point. There are detailed rehearsals of single speeches and of short scenes, experiments with playing styles, the *Speaker and listener* techniques of visualizing and mime in Act II, and a study of dramatic focus in Act I, illustrated by diagrams. While *Dramatic Methods* give a wide view of the play, these approaches aim at a con- centrated look at a smaller area to help the pupil to feel and understand poetical language and imagery. Both of these views are supported at various times by leading on to play material for a pair or group; there are group plays and mimes, *Missing scenes* and modern parallels. Some of these can be prepared and performed as easily as the Conversations, while others involve the whole class in a large space like a drama hall.

One of the great difficulties in reading a play is seeing the characters and the relationships between them in action; a mass of words lies between them and our understanding: we know what a character says, but not how he says it, how he feels, what he does with his face and hands, what kind of resistance there is between him and his listener. One approach to this problem is to open up the situation to a number of variations or deliberate distortions, each of which can be acted in two or three minutes in modern English, usually by two players. Each variation can be followed by a discussion which draws the student's attention to the real relationship, the actual characteriza- tion and how the plot depends on the characters' behaviour. These variations can be the basis of larger improvised plays in the drama hall, perhaps departing more radically from the original situation or the original characters.

In addition to this activity, there are some sections which deal specifically with the relationships between characters as they exist in the play. Principally, these concern the lovers' quarrels: Hermia–Demetrius, Helena–Demetrius, and Hermia–Helena. Other work deals with the different worlds of the mechanicals and the fairies.

Under the general heading of *Talking about acting* there

are reviews of productions at the Old Vic and Stratford as well as actors', playwrights' and directors' comments on the art of acting. The aim here is to provide another means of seeing the play, of looking at it from the professional viewpoint as the play in performance. This is a vital and often neglected area in the full understanding and enjoyment of the play.

Unlike the usual drama book, this book enables the student to draw on his normal study in English for all kinds of creative activity either as an individual working on a project or on written work, or as a member of a pair or group working on a private or public performance of ideas related to the original play. He is encouraged at all points to go back to the play for further study and research, for further information, as a check on the work he is doing, for movement, for character, and for close improvization, or to learn the script. By these means the less able student as well as the examination candidate may be led to a greater understanding and appreciation of a Shakespearian play.

A NOTE ON WORKING
How well should the student know the play before he uses this drama book for his practical work? The usual classes studying Shakespeare will probably read through the whole play first, possibly on their own, before beginning a detailed study with the teacher. It is at this point, as each scene is carefully examined, that practical work could begin. The teacher may, in some cases, encourage or ask his students to do their own research by preceeding his work on the text with their practical work. He may select students to prepare a particular piece for public performance and discussion; he may allow them a wide or even an unlimited choice; and he may want some work, whether set or chosen, to be prepared by all. Generally, however, he may feel that it is better for his students to use this drama book when they have a sound and secure basis

of detailed study on which to work.

When he is working with less able groups who may not have met Shakespeare before and now do so with reluctance, the teacher will naturally select a number of scenes which he feels will be reasonably well understood and enjoyed. From this point he might turn to a reading of the whole play or proceed to work on scenes in other plays. He may also gamble, and this can be very successful, on reading a more complex and apparently too difficult scene, and then reveal by his comments, by discussion and by performance how exciting and dramatically direct and effective it is. In either case he can offer his students a variety of practical work relating to the scenes that have been read.

It is also possible to approach the play through the drama book, when what students read and do stimulates interest in seeing the original text of the play. Some suggestions for group plays, for parallel improvization, some Conversations, the Playscripts and certain Montages could be worked on before the text is read. The teacher may simply outline the play's action and elaborate one particular situation; then, with pairs or groups, he begins practical work right away. The text is read afterwards and the practical work perhaps repeated with the original situation fresh in mind. The text should be available to those who want to refer to it during the first session of practical work.

The teacher may vary the above approach by reading through a scene with little or no commentary after his students have looked at the practical work they might do. Now they will have a very general picture of the play in mind, a fuller picture of one particular scene, an idea of what they have to do and some contact with the actual scene in the play. The scene which the teacher reads should be reasonably short or curtailed. The class is now equipped for its preliminary practical work.

Once students begin practical work some teachers may

feel unduly handicapped by their relative inexperience in handling acting in the classroom. Some may fear there may be more talk than work, or too much noise (for them, or for others, or for good results), or too much moving about in too limited a space. Some may fear that only the natural actors in the class will take part willingly; that there will be more watching, although this is valuable, than doing.

First of all a great deal of preparation can be done, and time saved and disturbance reduced to a minimum, outside the classroom in the students' own time. Work such as the 'Conversations for Two' can be quickly prepared without supervision; there are enough pieces for students to be able to find an aspect of the subject which interests them and which they will find easy enough or sufficiently challenging. As always, some students will dig deep into a situation and its characters while others will skim over a complex issue. But both should find that the suggested techniques and material lead them to a fresh view of Shakespeare because they are obliged to examine the text in a variety of ways.

For work which requires groups, and probably involves a good deal of movement, rehearsal time—again outside the classroom—should be set aside. Ideally, this work should be done in a Drama Hall under a drama specialist; otherwise groups must be left to work alone with occasional direction and advice from interested staff. Of course it is to be hoped that the English teacher himself, if he does not do so already, will feel that he could use some of his teaching time working with groups to explore some of the more detailed activities.

It is not essential that all, or even most, pieces of prepared work should be seen by the rest of the class. The play in performance, even a scene if it is fully prepared, needs an audience to give it full life; but most of the practical work in this book for pairs or small groups does not: it is designed for private performance, to be chosen, discussed, worked through, and played as a final version for the benefit of the players themselves. The teacher will check that the work is actually done; generally, the mere fact that the teacher is moving about listening, watching and asking questions will encourage those who always prefer to sleep in the sun. Private performance will release the diffident from the burden of having to act in front of the others while offering the responsibility of working together, of choice and of attainment. Some work should be seen in order to set standards and to open discussions.

There are two helpful keys here: the function and the duration of the activity. The teacher insists that the primary concern of himself and his students is not the standard of acting, but rather what light their efforts succeed in throwing upon the play. And it may be that the exercise just doesn't work for them, that it is unsuitable in some way. But points can be made and ideas expressed even when the acting is relatively weak—though it must be a sincere effort. In the Conversations some pairs will be hesitant and limited in their dialogue; but at the least it will be a verbal contribution which will improve with experience. Finally their performance of the simpler pieces at this stage is primarily concerned with only one aspect of acting, that is, speech, sometimes in character but often with the freedom of minor roles or modern parallels. The teacher also indicates that a performance of two or three minutes is all that is required for pair work and perhaps ten minutes for most group work. Under these conditions and with the stimulus of success, laughter and enjoyment, it will not be long before all the pairs are at least willing to perform.

As a general plan of procedure the teacher can follow this suggested sequence of work:

1 ask his class to prepare a Conversation or other piece of pair work for the next lesson.

2 perhaps also require written work suggested by the practical work or from the subjects suggested at the

end of each Act.

3   anyone without a partner, or whose partner is absent, should either work with a pair where that is possible or produce written work from the section under study or from the suggestions in *Imaginative written work*.

4   begin the following lesson by allowing pairs to revise their preparations.

5   watch a number of short performances.

6   open a discussion.

7   end with one or two performances repeated or played in a way which illustrates the points that emerged in the discussion.

On other occasions the teacher might suggest the writing of a script, in or out of the classroom, followed by a performance of the scripted play; this should preferably be learnt or closely improvised, but if it requires very little movement it can be read. Work can also be tape-recorded, prepared and taped outside the classroom by the pupils themselves, and played back during a lesson. This is another effective way of removing any reluctance to act. It might sometimes be possible to clear a large area of the classroom before the lesson begins and then to use all the time on group rehearsals.

As a starting point for the hesitant, teacher or student, simply turn to the appropriate Conversations and work along these lines:

1   these Conversations ask you to talk together in pairs about some of the material in the scene we have just been looking at. (It may be necessary to draw attention to several sets of Conversations where a long scene is divided into two or more sections.)

2   work with the person next to you; if there is anyone left over come and see me (when another spare player may be found or he can be told to join two other players).

3   read them through and choose one with your

partner. Then check back on the original text where you need to and quickly decide how you are going to do it. Play by talking quietly to one another —even if you're supposed to be shouting. You have ten minutes for all that. If you finish, either repeat your rehearsal or try another Conversation.

The teacher need say nothing about any kind of performance at this point; he may stress the need for working quietly while encouraging inventiveness and accepting laughter and the excitement of working something out for oneself. And if asked if they may act it for the others, he can suggest that that could be done later on. During this preparation he can walk round noting down which Conversation each pair is working on, and of course, use these brief contacts to offer help and to get the feel of how things are going. Then he may listen to a pair for a few moments and later may silence the class to listen for perhaps half a minute to a repetition of what he's just overheard; a brief comment and work goes on. No trumpets to announce performance. Before long he will know who can play a whole Conversation through successfully, who needs a little pressure to give something and who is so reluctant as to create general embarrassment. Here, of course, he can emphasise the value of private performance.

Finally a word about improvisation itself. In terms of drama it does not simply mean making it up as you go along, although this carries the idea. Basically it means playing a prepared situation with given characters without a script giving the actual dialogue; working from the information you have of character and plot, and sometimes of style, pace and mood, you make up suitable dialogue. This is free improvisation: the dialogue has a basic framework but there is no attempt to follow the original text. A close improvisation demands several rehearsals which work away from the free to almost a modern translation of the original text. At times this will be so close, or the passage will be so carefully studied, that various Shakespearian words and phrases will creep into the usual spoken English. Finally a polished improvisation —I use the word 'performance' to cover this—is simply an improvisation that has been developed as far as it will go, or as far as the players wish or are able to take it. The words will seem as if learnt from a script.

Throughout the New Penguin Shakespeare edition of *A Midsummer Night's Dream* has been used for quotations and line references.

WORKING METHODS

REFERENCES TO TEXT

All the scenes are divided into two or three sections with the exception of I ii and III i, which are treated as full units. The List of Contents shows this arrangement clearly.

At the beginning of each section, full references are given to Act, Scene, Section, and Line, and the characters are listed.

Each section is headed by a short quotation, as a title.

The reference to Act, Scene, and Section is also shown at the top of each page.

CONVERSATIONS FOR TWO

Conversations for two introduce every section by offering short situations related to the characters, the ideas, the action of the plot, the Elizabethan background, the mood, and themes.

These Conversations use invented characters, minor characters in the play and Elizabethans watching a performance of the play, as well as the principal characters themselves.

Some Conversations suggest modern situations in which you, as yourself, are involved.

You can play these Conversations without moving from your place, simply by turning and talking to the person next to you. The conversations can be quite short, perhaps only two or three minutes.

If you have enough space you can act these in the usual way, deciding by discussion where you are and what you are doing.

With some exceptions, which are noted, all the Conversations can be played by pairs of boys, pairs of girls or mixed pairs. Boys should attempt female roles and girls male roles, as well as roles for their own sex.

● This sign indicates the start of various activities for pair or group, and written work.

ACT ONE
Reality

DEMETRIUS . . . *Are you sure*
That we are awake?

———————•———————

ACT ONE
Scene 1

Thou hast . . .
Turned her obedience which is due to me
To stubborn harshness.

I i first section: from *Enter Theseus Hippolyta with others*,
to *Exeunt all but Lysander and Hermia* (l. 127)

THESEUS · HIPPOLYTA · EGEUS · PHILOSTRATE ·
LYSANDER · DEMETRIUS · HERMIA

———◆———

CONVERSATIONS FOR TWO

● The Duke sends his Master of Revels, Philostrate, to 'stir up the Athenian youth to merriments'. He is a solemn, elderly, pedantic state official. He meets Nick Bottom, earthy and full of life, who is very eager to celebrate the Duke's marriage. They have different ideas about suitable entertainments.

● Before going to see the Duke, Egeus appeals to his daughter Hermia for the last time to change her mind and agree to marry Demetrius. She insists she is in love with Lysander—why can't she be allowed to marry him? Egeus finally decides to take her before the Duke.

● Demetrius visits Egeus before this scene with the Duke. He wants to marry Hermia, although both he and Egeus know that she loves Lysander. Demetrius suggests that he is one of the Duke's favourites, and that this marriage would please the Duke.

● You want to marry a young man who is in love with you, but your father does not like him. He prefers another suitor and insists that you be sensible and marry him. You ask your mother to help you, but although she understands how you feel she does not want to go against your father.

● Unfortunately your two boy friends arrive at the house at the same time and neither will leave without the other. Each asks you to marry him, making all kinds of promises. You like each equally well, but you have to choose one. (Your partner plays both friends in turn.)

● You ask the father of your girl friend if you may marry her. He dislikes you intensely, as you know already; he scornfully asks what you have to offer, laughs at you and orders you out of the house. You struggle not to lose your temper but in the end there is a furious quarrel.

You can turn these Conversations into group plays by bringing in other characters and building up the story. Sometimes these can be made by using the material of two or three Conversations. Your new characters may not appear in fact in this part of the play, or they may not be in it at all. You are free to develop your own play in your own way.

The first Conversation is developed into a detailed group play on page 23.

You can turn these Conversations into scripts for two players or for a group. They can also be presented as newspaper reports or as short stories.

MISSING SCENE

Thou hast by moonlight at her window sung

LYSANDER · HERMIA · EGEUS · MOTHER

This 'missing' scene can be played in either a completely modern setting or in the setting of Shakespeare's play, both using modern English.

Lysander calls at Hermia's house during the evening; she slips out to see him and he gives her a present. She tells him that her father wants her to marry Demetrius, but she thinks that she might be able to make him change his mind, especially if her mother will help her. As they are arranging another meeting, Egeus comes out and drives Lysander away with threats and takes Hermia indoors.

The scene could continue indoors to show the conflict between father and daughter with the mother coming in and trying to act as peace-maker. We see how strongly Egeus is opposed to any marriage with Lysander and how determined and stubborn Hermia is.

Point of concentration: the opposition between love and reason.
To Egeus, Lysander's words and gifts have tricked his daughter into loving him. He can see, with the wisdom of age, that Lysander is not good enough for his daughter. Hermia, however, believes her feelings.

> HERMIA I would my father looked but with my eyes.
> THESEUS Rather your eyes must with his judgement look.

TALKING ABOUT ACTING 1

———•———

Behind the drama of words is the drama of action, the timbre of voice and voice, the uplifted hand or tense muscle, and the particular emotion. The spoken play, the words which we read, are symbols, a shorthand, and often, as in the best of Shakespeare, a very abbreviated shorthand indeed, for the acted and felt play, which is always the real thing. The phrase, beautiful as it may be, stands for a greater beauty still.

T. S. ELIOT from *Seneca in Elizabethan translation* Faber

———•———

Detailed rehearsals of one speech for 6 players and a Prompter
Physical language
Shakespeare could give dramatic expression to reactions, the characters' thoughts and feelings that lie beneath the

words that are spoken. Added to the verbal excitement is
the visual interest: we understand a great deal more by
seeing than by just hearing. We can read a gesture, a look,
a turn of the head, even a silence. Plays *can* be distorted by
irrelevant and trivial stage-business. We must look for the
gestures and business that can be implied from the text.

Exeunt is an important moment for business. Here is
Theseus' exit speech before he and the others depart
leaving the lovers, Hermia and Lysander, conveniently
together. It is followed by three practical Experiments
which illustrate how the text can be read with a visual eye
through the language of physical movement.

THESEUS

1   I must confess that I have heard so much,
    And with Demetrius thought to have spoke thereof;
    But, being overfull of self affairs,

2   My mind did lose it.

3   But Demetrius, come;
    And come, Egeus. You shall go with me.
    I have some private schooling for you both.

4   For you, fair Hermia, look you arm yourself
    To fit your fancies to your father's will;
    Or else the law of Athens yields you up—
    Which by no means we may extenuate—
    To death or to a vow of single life.

5   Come, my Hippolyta. What cheer, my love?

6   Demetrius and Egeus, go along;
    I must employ you in some business
    Against our nuptial, and confer with you
    Of something nearly that concerns yourselves.

                          I i. lines 111 to 126

Experiment One : Opening positions: Theseus and Hippolyta
seated with Egeus and Demetrius standing before them.
Hermia is a pace or two away from her father and on the
opposite side to Demetrius; a little from her is Lysander.

(Numbers refer to the speech as arranged on page 5.)

1   As Theseus begins his speech he rises to mark the end of the audience and joins Egeus and Demetrius. He speaks in a less official manner than formerly, casually, almost to himself.

2   'My mind did lose it.' He half turns and gives Hippolyta a brief smile.

3   He turns, friendly but businesslike to Demetrius and Egeus.

4   He moves across to Hermia, speaking quietly as if telling her to be sensible. Noting her hard expression, he issues a firm threat: 'Or else the law . . .' He pauses before reminding her that he will be unable to help her then.

5   Sensing her resistance, he turns away sharply to Hippolyta. His look and voice soften as he leads her from her seat; they smile at one another.

6   He remembers Egeus and Demetrius and cheerfully invites them to come with him. They go out together.

Experiment Two: Try out your own opening positions or use those in Experiment One. Look at the grouping of the characters from a distance, from the audience's point of view. What might they understand from the position of the players in relation to one another?

1   Whether seated or standing, Theseus begins in a bored, off-hand manner, waving the angry Lysander to silence—this is no time for quarrels. He pauses and smiles at Hippolyta on: 'But, being overfull of self affairs . . .'

2   'My mind did lose it.' His attention is taken up with Hippolyta: his voice drifts off into a soft and close whisper. She might reach up and touch his arm gently.

This show of affection is held for a moment so that Egeus smiles and coughs to remind Theseus that they are still there. Demetrius looks relieved.

3   When Egeus coughs, Theseus comes to them briskly with a lively, 'But Demetrius, come . . .' and a friendly hand on the shoulder.

4   He turns to Hermia and speaks to her as in Experiment
One. You can experiment with your own variations here.
5   He returns to where Hippolyta is sitting (or standing,
perhaps talking with Egeus) and takes her hand to lead
her off. For a moment, again, they are lost in one another
on: 'What cheer, my love?'
6   Once more brisk, but gay, he invites Egeus and
Demetrius to accompany them and they go out.

Experiment Three : Try out your own opening positions or
use those in Experiment One.
1   As Experiment Two. Theseus looks sharply at
Demetrius on: 'And with Demetrius thought to have
spoken thereof . . .' Egeus frowns for a moment, until he
sees that Theseus has forgotten the whole affair. Demetrius
looks very uncomfortable, emphasising the relief he feels
later. These words also sound a note of hope for Hermia
and Lysander: they might mark it by a quick glance at
each other.
2   As Experiment Two, but Egeus does not cough to
remind Theseus. The moment is held only long enough to
mark the reactions of each character. Egeus smiles kindly
on this open show of affection, appreciating how love
distracts from the cares of high office. Demetrius, while
relieved, is reminded of Hermia, and glances at her; she
does not look at him. Her slight hopes have been dashed
by this casual forgetfulness. She is tight with frustration
and anger. To Lysander, this is just what he expected:
'The course of true love never did run smooth.'
3   Theseus's friendly invitation disturbs Demetrius.
Hermia will be left alone with Lysander. He looks across
at her and Lysander as Theseus speaks; and his smile of
thanks is coldly formal. Egeus, of course, is delighted.
4   As Experiment One. Concentrate on the individual
reactions of Egeus, Demetrius and Lysander while
Theseus speaks to Hermia. Basically, they are all anxious
and tense. Note that Hermia does not reply. Theseus

7

might pause for a reply before turning away. Her answer is in her whole stance and eyes.

5 Theseus's first words, 'Come, my Hippolyta,' are a little cold and distant for a lover. He has still some of the harshness of his previous line in his mind. Hippolyta looks saddened by this change of mood, so that he draws closer with, 'What cheer, my love?' and she smiles with happiness.

6 Theseus repeats his invitation. Demetrius hesitates, looking at Hermia who does not see him. Egeus might touch his arm to call him along. Lysander realises that he and Hermia will be left alone and smiles a little at her. She might respond very briefly or remain lost in her own pain. The happy lovers and the others go out, Demetrius glancing back.

PLAYING THE EXPERIMENTS

Theseus speech should be learnt or closely improvised. You can also work with a prompter during rehearsals. He or she can read out each part of numbered speech as it is required, while the action is mimed by Theseus. After all, nobody else speaks during the Experiments.

Later, Theseus can repeat the prompter's words until he knows them. None of the six players should carry a book or act as prompter.

The Experiments should be tried in turn, the simplest, Experiment One, first. All the players should first read through the speech and all three Experiments before starting work.

Experiment One: Read through Sections 1 to 3 of the speech and items 1 to 3 of Experiment One. Leave books. Set up opening positions. Work through Sections 1 to 3 with the prompter helping with lines and reminders of actions when necessary.

Repeat this for the rest of the speech, Sections 4 to 6, and then run straight through.

Experiment Two: Use the same method as above.

Experiment Three: Use the same working method, but work on smaller Sections of the speech: 1 and 2, 3 and 4, 5 and 6.

Performance: The three Experiments can be shown to the class after rehearsals in a drama lesson or elsewhere. Discuss afterwards the differences in the performances and the effect of physical language on the understanding of the text.

———•———

So quick bright things come to confusion.

I i second section: from *Exeunt all but Lysander and Hermia* (l. 127) to *Enter Helena* (l. 179)

LYSANDER · HERMIA

———•———

CONVERSATIONS FOR TWO

● Lysander takes Hermia to his wealthy 'widow aunt'. Play this scene between Lysander and his aunt, with Hermia silent or also played by the person playing the aunt. She is delighted to see her adopted son, listens to the story of their elopement and promises to help them.

● Demetrius calls at Egeus' house. They discover that Hermia is not in the house and think that Lysander has taken her. They find a letter written by Hermia to her parents; it expresses her sorrow at leaving them, but also her determination to marry Lysander and not Demetrius.

● Hermia meets a close friend of her own age. Her friend is anxious to hear what happened at the Duke's house. She also finds out about the elopement plan, though Hermia is not very willing to tell her. Hermia knows that her friend loves romantic stories and is always passing on bits of gossip.

● Lysander meets a close friend of his own age, tells him what happened at the Duke's, and of his elopement plan. Lysander's friend is rather timid and conventional; he begs Lysander to think again and not to displease the Duke. He points out that Hermia is virtually under sentence of death if she does not obey her father, and disobedience would include a runaway marriage.

GROUP PLAY
The Elopement
All the ideas suggested in the Conversations above are brought together in this play. It is in the form of a romantic comedy, like *A Midsummer Night's Dream* itself: a play of intrigue, of lovers meeting and rivals plotting and of others hindering the course of true love.

Most of the incidents are not Shakespeare's, though they are suggested by him, but most of the characters are his, and should be played in character. The main thing is to show the kinds of love: parental love, the love of friends, jealousy, devotion and true love.

THE ELOPEMENT
A Romantic Comedy for 4 boys and 4 girls

LYSANDER · HIS FRIEND · EGEUS · DEMETRIUS · HERMIA · HER FRIEND · HER MOTHER

HELENA
THE WIDOW AUNT } one player

Place: various; indicate in dialogue

PLAN OF ACTION
1 Hermia and Lysander agree to elope that night. They will make their way through the woods to Lysander's widow aunt.
2 On his way home, Lysander meets a friend and tells him of the Duke's decision and of the elopement. His friend is very much against this (see Conversations, p. 10) and they go off arguing.

3   On her way home, Hermia meets a friend who extracts all the news from her (see Conversations, p. 9), and promises not to breathe a word. Hermia goes home.

4   Hermia's friend meets Helena and eagerly tells her everything. At first Helena is delighted. With her rival out of the way perhaps Demetrius will think about her again. She promises to say nothing and they part.

5   At home, Hermia tells her mother about her terrible time with the Duke and begs her to make her father change his mind; her mother is sympathetic but feels it would be better if she obeyed her father. Egeus comes in, angry with Hermia's behaviour before the Duke. Hermia goes to her room, now determined to elope.

6   Egeus and his wife quarrel over Hermia, she trying to get him to understand Hermia's feelings, and he insisting that the whole matter has been settled and that he will not give in to her silly ideas. She'll be quite happy with Demetrius, and his wife has to agree that there's nothing wrong with him.

7   Helena finds Demetrius and tells him about the elopement. (See I i. lines 246 to 251.) The news makes him very angry; then he suspects a trick. Why is she telling him? He cannot believe she is doing it out of love. He drags her off with him to Egeus' house to make sure.

8   Hermia's friend sees Demetrius and Helena going off together and realises that her gossip has lead to this betrayal. She sees Lysander's friend, explains things to him and they rush off to find Lysander at once.

9   Demetrius and Helena arrive at Egeus' house. The parents do not believe a word of the elopement story. Helena feels very stupid and embarrassed. They look for Hermia, without success, but they find a letter she has left (see Conversations, p. 9).

10   Lysander and his two friends reach the garden of the house. Through the windows they see Demetrius; they are too late! Lysander is in despair, the girl weeps because she has spoilt everything, and the friend tries to console

Lysander by saying that it's all for the best: at this moment Hermia comes out of her hiding place in the garden.

11   Suddenly they are seen from the windows. Egeus will rouse the guards and their escape will be prevented. Lysander's friend offers to stay behind while the others run off. Hermia's friend stays with him. The lovers run off. The boy sends the girl running off in the opposite direction and when Egeus and the others reach him, directs them after the girl.

12   Lysander and Hermia reach the safety of his widow aunt's house and are greeted joyfully. (See Conversations, p. 9). They tell her the whole story and she promises to help them.

PLAYING STYLES
As well as playing *The Elopement* in a modern, natural way as in everyday life, it can also be played as a farce by speeding up the many exits and entrances and by some exaggeration of character and speech.

It will also work as a melodrama, giving suitable weight to the father and using Demetrius as the villain with Helena as his accomplice.

WRITTEN WORK
A script can be written using any of these three playing styles. Keep the particular style in mind while you are writing.

Love looks not with the eyes, but with the mind,
And therefore is winged Cupid painted blind.

I i third section: from *Enter Helena* (l. 179) to end
LYSANDER · HERMIA · HELENA

CONVERSATIONS FOR TWO

● Helena tells Demetrius about Hermia's intention to elope with Lysander. He cannot understand why Helena should tell him, although she says she does it because she loves him. He blames Lysander for this plan; he will not believe that Hermia wants to marry Lysander. He storms off angrily to stop them.

● Before these unhappy times, Hermia and Helena used to meet in the woods to exchange stories about their boy friends. Helena has just met Demetrius, and Hermia has met Lysander, and the path of true love seems very smooth.

● At one time Demetrius was happy with Helena, with no thoughts of Hermia. He exchanges stories of true love and eternal happiness with Lysander. Jokingly, they compare the two girls, even suggesting swopping partners for a while.

● Until now, Demetrius has been in love with Helena; now he has met Hermia, and his feelings towards Helena begin to change. He meets Helena and tries to explain as kindly as he can. She knows he is different, but she hopes it is only a moment's fancy. So she pretends not to understand what he is saying and reminds him of all their happy times together.

● Like Helena, you suddenly find that your boy friend is suddenly more interested in your best friend, although she does not like him at all and has her own boy friend. You ask her to help you get him back and work out a way of doing this between you.

● Hermia has told Lysander that she is being pestered by his friend Demetrius. Lysander tells him to leave her alone and think about Helena. He doesn't believe that Demetrius really loves Hermia; he either wants to make Helena jealous because they've quarrelled, or he's doing it out of spite to him. They part, still quarrelling.

TALKING ABOUT ACTING 2

———————◆————

What is the art of acting? . . . It is the art of embodying the poet's creations, of giving them flesh and blood, of making the figures which appeal to your mind's eye in the printed drama live before you on the stage. 'To fathom the depths of character, to trace its latent motives, to feel its finest quiverings of emotion, *to comprehend the thoughts that are hidden under the words*, and thus possess one's self of the actual mind of the individual man'— such was Macready's definition of the player's art.

HENRY IRVING

———————◆————

HELENA AND HERMIA: RELATIONSHIPS
In matters of love can you trust even your best friend?

'What's so marvellous about her? What's wrong with me? She's a flirt, that's it. You wouldn't expect your best friend to do that to you, would you? We've known each other since we were kids—just like sisters—told each other everything, shared everything; just like now, except that she's doing all the sharing. Perhaps you never really get to know some people. Oh, she's not like that—it's me! She's got her own boy, Lysander. She's in love with him. She doesn't want Demetrius. I wouldn't want Lysander hanging round me all the time! Unless . . . she likes all the attention she gets. Oh, yes! How nice to have two boys falling over themselves for you! And it makes Lysander a bit jealous and keeps him interested! Aren't you a clever little thing!'

Does Helena's thinking run along these lines? Or does she trust her little friend so completely that hardly a jealous, let alone a suspicious thought enters her head?

THE SEARCH FOR INNER LIFE
The words themselves will provide some of the answers to

our questions about Hermia and Helena. We can note their character in this scene and others in the play. We can watch performances of the play and see how these roles are interpreted by professional players. And we can make the search ourselves by playing the two parts in various ways. The words can be learnt or improvised closely or in quite free modern English.

Three interpretations of the relationship

Text *from* HERMIA God speed, fair Helena! Whither away?
to HERMIA That he hath turned a heaven unto a hell?

lines 180 to 207

WORKING METHOD

Read through the interpretations below and select one to begin on. Read through the original text.

Improvise the scene between you very freely in modern English. Check the interpretation and play through again.

Either improvise closer to the text *or* begin work on another interpretation.

● Play Hermia as a sweet little scatter-brained innocent. She hasn't a thought in the world, and certainly none to hurt Helena. Demetrius's devotion to her simply alarms and amazes her; in fact, to her wholesome mind, it is not quite nice: proper and true love needs only one boy and one girl.

Not having suffered in love, she doesn't know how hurt you can be by it. So even when she's being kind and sympathetic (lines 194 to 202) she carelessly says too much and wounds Helena unintentionally.

Against this interpretation, play Helena as a more thoughtful and aggressive girl, deeply hurt by the loss of Demetrius and by the fact that it is her friend who has taken him from her. It wasn't done deliberately, but it still leaves her feeling envious and humiliated. Bewildered, but still sensible, she wants to know why all this happened.

Begin the scene: Hermia greets her friend brightly, glad to see her again, and with no idea of her misery. Helena doesn't want to talk to her; she doesn't want to talk to anyone, except Demetrius, so she begins aggressively.

● Play Hermia as pretending to be all sweetness and innocence. Remember that Lysander is there (whether you actually have a player there or not). In reality she is determined to get just what she wants. She will not marry Demetrius; she will run away from home with her choice; and she can show Lysander that he's lucky to get her. To her, Helena is a nice enough girl but she doesn't know how to keep a boy interested. Really it serves her right; anyway, she can have him back now she's leaving.

Against this interpretation, play Helena as a girl of lively spirit and intelligence who is quite able to see through her friend's little tricks. She's certainly not going to let her see how hurt she is. No: she'll play her at her own game and simply ask her how she does it. Perhaps Lysander will see what a vain and jealous little flirt she is.

Begin the scene: Hermia is being as nice as possible to Helena, who responds with smiles and laughter and praise for Hermia's attractiveness.

● Play Hermia as being acutely embarrassed by the whole business. The last thing she wants is Lysander to think that she has encouraged Demetrius in any way. She certainly hasn't, and doesn't want to. Now Helena comes along and makes her look guilty. She protests her innocence vigorously, trying to convince them both.

Helena is furious with Hermia. She is quite certain that, for some reason, Hermia has encouraged Demetrius. After all, why should he suddenly leave her and run after Hermia? Here's a chance to show her up in front of Lysander for what she is.

Begin the scene with a nervous greeting from Hermia. She retreats before Helena's furious accusations. Helena makes sure Lysander notices these. She speaks rapidly, and doesn't give Hermia a chance to make excuses.

PLAYING THE SCENE

Even if you learn the words and then play out these interpretations you will find that the character's hidden thoughts and feelings will affect how you say the words, how you look and what you do.

It is vital to remember that Lysander is present all the time. Whichever interpretation you take, it would be different if he were not there, partly because the words would be different (see Projects at the end of Act) and because Helena and Hermia could express their real feelings more freely.

Three players: HERMIA · HELENA · LYSANDER

Bring Lysander into your scene to see what effect he has in performance, although he says very little.

In the first interpretation Lysander is reasonably sympathetic towards Helena. He treats her as a good friend who has been made undeservedly miserable.

In the second, Lysander begins to see Hermia in a less favourable light. This is a side of her he hasn't seen before. Has she been encouraging Demetrius behind his back? Surely Helena is just envious of their happiness.

In the third, Lysander is astonished by Helena's anger and perhaps protects Hermia as Helena rushes at her. But she couldn't be so angry without reason. There's no smoke without . . . No, Helena's just mad with jealousy.

DRAMATIC METHOD

Soliloquy

At the end of the first scene Helena is left alone on the stage to speak her thoughts aloud. Bottom is the only other character to do this, in IV i. All our attention is focused on her. Why?

You will be able to supply several reasons from the text. Is there another which can be made more apparent in performance? The framework for Helena's thoughts is:

a brief thought of the happiness of some lovers
thoughts about her own situation
thoughts about the nature of love: how it affects behaviour
thoughts about her own painful experience
decision: to betray her friend because of her love

WORKING METHOD
Pair work: using the framwork for Helena's thoughts. Whether improvising closely or freely, keep this famework in mind. Text: I i lines 226–251.

First part: Girls Helena and partner
                         Hermia and partner
                         Hermia's mother and partner

Second part: Boys Demetrius and partner
                         Lysander and partner
                         Egeus and partner

Girls

● Helena and a silent partner who simply listens to the improvisation of this speech, discusses it with the player and then tries it herself.
● Helena and a silent partner who acts as a 'mirror' to her thoughts and feelings. She can work in very small mime, using just face and hands while sitting in front of Helena. Or she can work in full mime using all the body in a dance-drama.
● Helena and a partner with similar experiences in love. Helena is still the more active of the two, but her partner confirms and supports everything she says from her own experience, improvising her own dialogue.
● Helena and a partner in opposition. This should not be argument between the players. It should express two opposite points of view about love, about Helena's situation and about what she should do now. Although the players must respond to each other's thoughts, Helena, in

particular, must concentrate on her own feelings and not lose this concentration by becoming angry or irritated with her partner as a person.

We can also look at the ideas expressed in this speech through Hermia's eyes:

● Hermia and silent partner. Hermia follows the framework of Helena's speech, but it expresses her own experience of the nature of love, her thoughts about her elopement, the painful disagreement with her father and her defiance of Theseus, and finally her decision to go with Lysander. Her partner listens to this improvisation, discusses it and then tries it herself.

● Hermia and 'mirror' partner, as for Helena.

● Hermia and partner in agreement, as for Helena. Remember that this is *not* a conversation between the players.

● Hermia and partner in opposition, as for Helena. Respond to each other's argument, but do not become personally involved.

The older and more experienced generation has something to say about the nature of love. We can look through the eyes of Hermia's mother. As a starting point, we can imagine that she doesn't mind who her daughter marries as long as she is happy, and although she doesn't like the way her husband, Egeus, has handled things, she will not openly oppose him.

● Hermia's mother and silent partner. She follows the same framework of Helena's speech, but expresses her more experienced view of the nature of love. She begins by thinking about her daughter's happiness and whether it will make much difference whom she marries, Demetrius or Lysander. Then her general ideas about love and marriage, her own experience, especially her quarrels with Egeus over Hermia, and finally her decision to support her husband's ideas.

● Hermia's mother and 'mirror' partner.

● Hermia's mother and partner in agreement.
● Hermia's mother and partner in opposition.

Boys
We can look at the ideas expressed in Helena's soliloquy
from a male point of view, through the eyes of Demetrius,
Lysander and Egeus. Each follows the framework of
Helena's speech.
● Demetrius and silent partner who simply listens to his
improvisation, discusses it and then tries it himself.
Demetrius, like Helena, can look at the happiness of others
in love and compare it with his own situation of being
hated by the girl he loves, and loved by the girl he now
hates. From this he gives his own ideas about the nature
of love, recalls again his own experience and Hermia's
public refusal to marry him, and decides never to give up.
● Demetrius and a silent partner who acts as a mirror to
his thoughts and feelings. Partner can work in very small
mime, using just hands and face while sitting in front of
Demetrius. Or he can work in full mime, using all the body
in a dance-drama.
● Demetrius and a partner in agreement with his thoughts
and feelings. Demetrius is still the more active, but the
partner confirms and supports everything he says about
his experiences by improvising his own dialogue.
● Demetrius and partner in opposition. This should not
be an argument between the players. It should express
opposite views about love, and about Demetrius' situation
and what he should do now. Demetrius must concentrate
on his own feelings and not become angry with his partner
as a person.
● Lysander and silent partner who listens, discusses and
then improvises. Lysander begins with thoughts of his
present happiness, then of the dangers and difficulties of
eloping with Hermia, and so to his own view of the nature
of love. He remembers the painful scene with the Duke
and Egeus, the trouble that Demetrius has caused by

falling out of love with Helena, and decides to risk everything and elope.

● Work with partner as above: mirror; partner in agreement; partner in opposition.

● Egeus and silent partner. Egeus, like Hermia's mother, expresses a more experienced view of the nature of love. He begins by thinking about his own happy marriage now disturbed by quarrels over his disobedient daughter. He is certain that Demetrius is a far more suitable husband for her than Lysander. Then he comments on the nature of love and marriage in general, recalls the embarrassing scene before the Duke and the scornful attitude of Lysander and determines that Hermia will marry Demetrius and no one else.

● Work with partner as above: mirror; partner in agreement; partner in opposition.

ACT ONE
Scene II

I will aggravate my voice so that I will
roar you as gently as any sucking dove.

I ii whole scene

PETER QUINCE · NICK BOTTOM · FRANCIS FLUTE ·
TOM SNOUT · ROBIN STARVELING · SNUG

———————●———————

CONVERSATIONS FOR TWO

● Nick Bottom calls on Peter Quince to tell him about
Philostrate's suggestion that the craftsmen devise some
entertainment for the Duke. (The first of the Conversations on page 2 deals with the visit of the Master of
Revels.) While Bottom is enormously enthusiastic and full
of ideas, he finds old Quince very reluctant and full of
doubts and difficulties.

● The wives of Bottom and Quince exchange the latest
gossip about the Duke's forthcoming wedding, Egeus'
trouble with his daughter, and their husbands' mad idea
of performing a play—of all things!—before the Duke.

● Snug, who is 'slow of study' and young Flute who has 'a
beard coming' and is easily embarrassed, discuss Bottom's
suggestion that the craftsmen perform a play. They are not
at all anxious to take part, but they don't want to let their
mates down. After they have been given their parts, they
meet again. They would much rather let Bottom play their
parts as he said he wanted to.

● Bottom's wife tries to persuade him not to do the play.
He will make a fool of himself and all his friends in front of
'all those rich folk'. And what will the neighbours think?
He ought to be working, not wasting his time with play-
acting! Bottom is so lost in the wonder of becoming an

actor and so full of his abilities that he is amazed at her failure to see the splendour of the occasion, and his genius.

TALKING ABOUT ACTING 3

The craftsmen

The workmen were allowed all the traditional bits of funny business, yet somehow all remained human and lovable . . . one remembers especially Paul Daneman's fussy, managing Quince, Daniel Thorndike's stone-deaf, aged and perplexed Starveling, Derek Francis' stolid, silent and well-meaning Snout, and Ronald Fraser's simple Flute, cause of most of the chaos in the play scene. Frankie Howerd succeeded perfectly in making Bottom the Weaver an acceptable colleague of the others. He might be filled with inexpressible scorn at their stupidities, outraged by their folly in spoiling one of his big scenes, and convinced that he could perform all offices better than any of them—but he was essentially one of the company and there was something so endearing about him that their sadness at his supposed disappearance became quite touching.

MARY CLARKE reviewing Michael Benthall's 1957 production at the Old Vic; *Shakespeare at the Old Vic 5* Hamish Hamilton

GROUP PLAY

The Play review makes a useful guide for the playing of this scene (I ii) and the other craftsmen scenes. These notes do not indicate the only way or the best way of playing the craftsmen; they are intended as a starting point for experiment and discussion.

The group play, *A Part to Tear a Cat in*, is arranged to show something of the working life of Bottom and his friends, the awe which the pompous magnificence of the Master of Revels inspires in them (though perhaps not in

Bottom), their natural fear of making fools of themselves before rich and important people—a sense of the difference of class—and their knowledge that they are not even practised amateur actors.

A Part to Tear a Cat in
A comedy for nine players

PHILOSTRATE, the Duke's Master of Revels
PETER QUINCE   cast as Thisbe's father
NICK BOTTOM   ,,   Pyramus
FRANCIS FLUTE   ,,   Thisbe
TOM SNOUT   ,,   Pyramus' father
ROBIN STARVELING ,,   Thisbe's mother
SNUG, the joiner   ,,   the lion
PETER QUINCE'S WIFE
NICK BOTTOM'S WIFE
Other women may be added
Note: in the actual performance Quince is Prologue and Prompter, Snout is Wall, and Starveling is Moonshine.

Place: the craftsmen's workshops; the yard of Peter Quince's house.

PLAN OF ACTION
1   The craftsmen working at their various trades in their shops. The two wives meet in the street and exchange gossip about the Duke's forthcoming wedding (see Conversations, p. 22) and Egeus' trouble with his daughter.
2   Peter Quince completes a chair and goes off to deliver it. He passes the workshops of the other craftsmen and greets each of them by name. As he goes out. Philostrate, the Master of Revels, comes in.
3   Philostrate asks the wives for Master Quince's house. He gives no reason why he wants to see him. Quince's wife is thrown into nervous confusion by Philostrate's appearance, his solemn manner and his request. Bottom's wife, once she has got over her initial surprise, assumes a very

grand manner and makes sure that everyone can see what fine company she keeps.

4 Philostrate is given a seat in the yard of Quince's house. Quince's wife dashes off to find him while Bottom's wife offers him something to drink which he politely but firmly refuses. Then she rushes off to her husband's shop to tell him what has happened.

5 Bottom introduces himself to Philostrate. He is polite and respectful, but he is not overwhelmed as the wives are. When Philostrate insists that he must speak to the senior craftsman, Bottom points out that although he is not the senior man he is—well, the spokesman, the natural leader.

6 As Philostrate is becoming increasingly irritated by the curious stares and comments of passers-by and the other craftsmen, he explains that the Duke wishes him to arrange some merry entertainment to celebrate his marriage. Bottom is delighted. They will perform a play —a famous, classical play!

7 Philostrate feels that he ought to speak to all the players, to impress on them the high honour the Duke is bestowing on them. Bottom goes to fetch them. His wife follows him, arguing that all he will do is make a fool of himself and his friends (see Conversations, p. 22).

8 He calls his friends out from their shops, but before he can explain everything to them Quince and his wife hurry in. So he explains it all to him with everyone else hanging on to his excited, colourful version of the events. Old Quince is put out by Bottom's acting as the senior man and nervous about meeting Philostrate. He raises all sorts of cautious doubts and difficulties (see Conversations, p. 22).

9 The craftsmen and wives troop off to Quince's yard where Philostrate is hot and irritable from his long wait in the sun. He explains again, with some cheerful help from Bottom, the Duke's request, the importance of the occasion, the high honour done to them, the high standard expected, the possibility of some small token of the Duke's thanks; and he will attend one of their rehearsals.

10   Before he leaves, Philostrate gives Quince the play parts he brought with him. The craftsmen are so excited and curious about the play that they ignore Philostrate's impatient departure. They begin to cast it immediately, although Snug and Flute are not very keen to take part (see Conversations, p. 22).

The play can continue with an improvisation of the original scene, perhaps also bringing in the two wives, who are firmly against the whole ridiculous idea.

FOCUS IN ACT ONE

In watching a play in the theatre—any play, in any theatre—
we sometimes sit forward in our chair, head forward and eyes
intent on one particular point in the arena or picture which is
the stage; this kind of dramatic focus is intense, concentrated.
We observe or watch for the minutest action or word; we often
see only one particular person or hear only one particular
sound, even though the stage may be crowded or noisy or
disorderly. The opposite extreme is a wide dramatic focus.
Instead of sitting forward we are sometimes relaxed, sitting
back, and responsive to the whole picture. At such a time no
one person or sound or action dominates the impression we
receive; we are sitting back and 'taking it all in'; we are
conscious of the overall effect, of the interweaving of pattern
and the range of colour. It is a wide focus. We can become
aware of a changing dramatic focus by marking these two
extremes.

J. R. BROWN *Shakespeare's Plays in Performances* Penguin

DRAMATIC METHOD

Focus—the changing shape of the stage

The View Localized

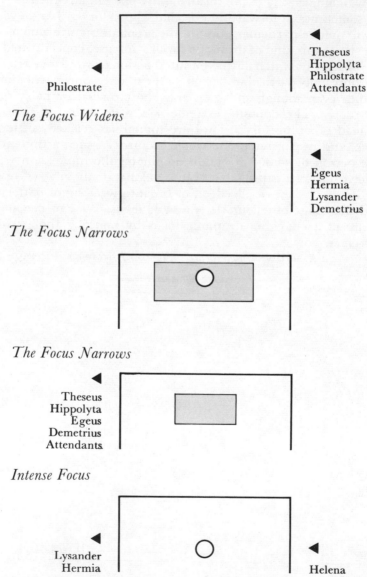

The Focus Widens

The Focus Narrows

The Focus Narrows

Intense Focus

The first Act is over. In terms of performance, what has happened? What have we seen?

The view localized

Before Theseus and Hippolyta enter we can see the stage setting and hear courtly music and laughter. Now we note the rich clothes and aristocratic bearing, the deference of the courtiers and the authority of Theseus with his command to Philostrate. But it is not a solemn occasion: faces and words are bright with the happiness of love.

The focus widens

With the entry of four more characters of obvious wealth and importance, the stage picture widens and then becomes more static for the serious business of the dispute.

The focus narrows

Our attention is now directed to Theseus who listens to the dispute and gives his judgment. On the crowded stage Theseus remains the dramatic focus until, with his exit with the court, the stage picture shrinks to the intimate world of Lysander and Hermia. Now the mood is less formal and the pace quickens as they plan their elopement. These two kinds of focus are shown in the third and fourth diagrams.

Intense focus

Helena's entrance heightens the dramatic tension. In her conversation with Hermia we see how much she has suffered. But when she is left alone the intense focus takes us inside the character, revealing the hurt and the jealousy, the devotion and the betrayal. In contrast to the earlier wide focus we move from a general outside view to a particular inside view.

Wide focus

In the following scene the focus widens again to that of the whole stage picture for the contrasting mood of the robust humour of the mechanicals. (This is not shown in the diagrams.)

PROJECT ONE

Class Work The effect of this dramatic method of changing focus can only be gauged by performing and by watching. The first Act can be closely improvised or learnt in its complete form, or carefully cut. The class should be split into two casts, so that each can perform and each can watch. There are 14 parts, not including attendants (who can be doubled) so everyone can be involved.

Points of Concentration: the changing focus; what is learnt from each stage picture; moments of intense focus: Theseus' speech and Helena; contrast between Court and mechanicals; variations of playing speed, between pictures and within each picture.

PROJECT TWO

Pair work Prepare a similar series of diagrams illustrating changing focus for any of the other Acts or Scenes in this play. Complete this with your own commentary. This project can be done before the particular Act is seen (on the stage) and your reading can be compared with the actual performance. You may be wrong. Similarly a performance can be examined afterwards against your interpretation of the text.

If the Act, or the whole play, has been seen by the class, this project can form the basis of a class discussion, with the diagrams drawn on the blackboard. Other pairs could bring forward counterviews of the stage picture.

Imaginative written work

Scripts may be written by one or more pupils working together. It is better to write the script after the play has been improvised.

● A script for any of the Conversations in this Act for either two players or enlarged for group playing.
● A script for the Missing Scene on page 3. Improvise the scene or scenes before writing.

● A script for *The Elopement*, pages 10 to 12. Split up the actions of this play amongst individuals or pairs in the group for writing.

● A script for *A Part to Tear a Cat in* on pages 24 to 26. Split up the actions amongst the group for writing after improvising the play.

● A script for Hermia's quarrel with her father, Egeus, arranged as a modern play where the girl's father refuses to let her marry the man of her choice. Other characters can be introduced into the story as required. The father can threaten to make his daughter a ward of court in order to prevent the marriage.

● Write a new scene between Helena and Hermia for the conversation between them which might occur if Lysander was not present. This scene is described in detail on pages 14 to 17.

● Select part of a scene from this Act (perhaps only one or two speeches, like Theseus' speech on page 5) and describe a detailed rehearsal of it. It is best to actually rehearse the selected passages, make notes, and write your rehearsal plan afterwards.

● Look at the examples of Play Review given under the general heading of *Talking About Acting,* and write a review of part or all of this Act after you have seen a performance of it.

ACT TWO
Confusion

HELENA . . . *Apollo flies, and Daphne holds the chase;*
The dove pursues the griffin; the mild hind
Makes speed to catch the tiger

———————•———————

ACT TWO
Scene I

I am that merry wanderer of the night.

II i first section, from *Enter a Fairy and Puck*
to *Enter Oberon . . . Titania* (l. 59)

PUCK · FAIRY

———————————— ● ————————————

CONVERSATIONS FOR TWO

● You are the 'wisest aunt' telling a very sad story of your misfortunes and those of your friends and relatives to another old dear. She is becoming rather bored with all the accidents, illnesses and deaths you recall, and irritated with your wise old recipes for good health. Besides, she can't get a word in edgeways—until you fall off a stool. Now she can be wise after the event.

● A 'gossip' and her friend are drinking cider and exchanging stories about magic and witchcraft. The gossip is a good down-to-earth body who scoffs at all this magic nonsense. Her friend urges her not to say such things, you never know who might be listening, some funny things do happen. When the gossip very nearly chokes on a crab-apple in her drink, they are both frightened. For a while the gossip believes that there might be something in it after all.

● Two Elizabethan workmen stagger home merrily after a long evening's drinking at The Boar's Head Inn. The night holds no fears for them until they fall over a farm gate that shouldn't be there. Then they recall their frothless ale and how they laughed at stories of Hobgoblins. They run and lose their way, circling the same haystack three times, bumping into one another to their mutual alarm, and hearing, it seems, the laughter of the devil.

● This can be played by boys or girls. You come across Puck in his leather clothes in the woods. He appears to be as solid and as ordinary as you are, but there are, you notice, some curious differences. Anyway, you don't believe in fairies or magic so he must be dressed up for some party or to advertise something. Still, if he insists he is Puck or Robin Goodfellow or whatever, let him prove it. His disappearing act is pretty good; but it's really only a clever trick. It's not until you're transformed that you're convinced.

DRAMATIC METHOD

The supernatural
In an instant the whole texture of the play changes. From the world of the Court and the confusions of romantic love we were plunged, without warning, into the earthy workaday world of the craftsmen; now, with equal suddeness, and in striking contrast to Bottom's world, we are in a new world composed of moonlight, flowers, fountains and dewdrops, inhabited by fairies.

So much we can gain from the text for ourselves. But the modern mind finds it very difficult to accept this world: fairies belong to childhood, to sixpence under the pillow, to pantomime. Few Elizabethans felt any doubts about the real existence of the supernatural world. King James himself published a book on demonology in 1597, upholding the real existence of warlocks and witches.

While we cannot believe, we can work towards an imaginative acceptance of this secret world around us. Such a step is vital to our full understanding and enjoyment of the play. Shakespeare gives us the clue when Theseus and Hippolyta watch the craftsmen's efforts to deal with material which they did not accept or understand:

HIPPOLYTA This is the silliest stuff that ever I heard.

35

THESEUS   The best in this kind are but shadows; and the
           worst are no worse, if imagination amend them.
HIPPOLYTA It must be your imagination, then, and not theirs.

The actors of the interlude need the imaginative participation of the stage-audience. The whole play needs our imagination, our willing acceptance of the dramatic illusion. It is what, after all, every play demands; *A Midsummer Night's Dream* simply makes greater demands.

VERBAL DRAMA
The problem remains how to become imaginatively involved in the play and in this fairy world in particular.

Like Shakespeare we must create imaginatively through the words. They must be heard, felt in the blood, understood with the inner ear like a piece of music. The printed word on the page will remain a mere symbol for most of us until we begin to begin to explore its power.

WORKING METHOD
The working method that follows is used for work on non-dramatic speeches which may appear to be mere decoration or scene-setting; in reading, the eye and the mind are likely to skip nimbly over them to the more obviously dramatic text.

The work is designed for two players, boys, girls or one of each, who can read the text during rehearsal and during performance if it is not known by heart by then. It will be seen that the text is read by the partner while the other performs so that the book does not get in the way.

As far as possible each pair should work on its own and no pair should have an audience during its rehearsals. As considerable concentration is required, movement and noise must be kept to a minimum; if a hall is used, use the floor for sitting rather than chairs.

Stages of work : listening
                 visualizing
                 hand mime

            continuous movement mime
            face
            whole body (individual or pair)

Further stages: with an observer
                with a 'deaf' person
                with a 'blind' person
                with a 'mirror'

It is not necessary to work through all these stages for any one speech. For later work, select those which interest you or lead you to successful work.

Pair work: boys/girls
Fairy's speech, lines 2 to 17

● One player reads the speech aloud to his or her partner, who sits with eyes shut, listening. Discuss the reading and the experience of listening in this way, repeat or change over parts.

The aim is to hear the words as if for the first time, concentrating upon them without interruption or distraction. You may comment, perhaps, on any word or phrase or image that you hadn't noticed in reading it yourself.

● As above, one reading while the other listens with eyes shut, visualizing the images called up by the words. The reading should be a little slower than normal. Discuss the reading and the experience of visualizing words. Repeat or change over parts.

The aim is to allow the words to create a total impression of this world by the listener building up a series of personal pictures. You may discuss particularly vivid images or where you found it difficult to see.

● While one reads, the partner uses hand mime to convey the images. The reading must be taken slowly at first; that is, with frequent pauses to allow the partner to work out or develop the image-gesture. The reading should not be interrupted by any comment or discussion between the players; nor does the reader watch his partner except to judge the pauses. This first mime should be a personal expression of the images.

The aim is to transform the words into physical language, as used by the deaf. At first it is sufficient if the performer makes this language clear to himself. Discussion can now follow, and the player can repeat the mime or the parts can be changed.

● This is a development of the hand-mime above. During the reading, the performer tries to achieve a continuous flow of movement with his hands, pausing only to mark the major changes in the speech. During these pauses the hands should not be dropped or changed from their last position. The reading must also be flowing and continuous, and now the reader must watch the performer so as to adjust his reading, particularly the speed, to the performer's movements. The performer is now in control.

The aim here is to reflect the subtleties of the verse-rhythms by the flowing movements of the hands, marked and emphasised by the held pauses and stronger gestures.

CONCENTRATION

This kind of work demands the whole attention of reader and performer. Both are involved in the unfamiliar processes of fully absorbed listening and visualizing. Both must, to begin with, be physically still and comfortable; then there must be an inner stillness and silence. Then the work of imaginative involvement can begin.

One help is music. This can either be selected by the teacher for the whole class, or, where possible, be an individual choice. It should be an instrumental piece, one that enables you to create this new world.

Pair work on other speeches
Use the Working Method described on page 36.

● Puck's speech: 'The King doth keep his revels here tonight', lines 18 to 31.

A more dramatic piece, essentially story-telling, but

player and reader should note the changes of mood: the opening gaiety of the King's revels, then his anger; Titania's love for the changeling; the contrasting harshness of Oberon—his jealousy, his knights, the wild forest; then, once again, all the beauty and magic of this world; a final discordant note, and the fearful elves creeping away to hide.

● The Fairy's second speech: 'Either I mistake your shape and making quite'

. This is full of fun on a more human scale. Reading and mime should convey this lively lightness. The performer can catch it in the quicker, dancing movements of his hands and, of course, reflect the humour in his face. This doesn't mean the idiot's grin but the expression of alarm for the frightened maids, the worried puffing for the breathless housewife churning away, the drunken fear of the night-wanderers.

● Puck's speech: 'Thou speakest aright: I am that merry wanderer of the night'

This is full of the earthy vigour of his fun. Each incident is easy to visualize and to depict in hand-mime. Again the performer's face is part of the mime, especially in dealing with the story of the 'wisest aunt'. Here is the straight-faced opening, her look round for the stool, her surprise and alarm when she falls, her coughing; and then the face breaks into a smile and builds to spluttering laughter and beaming congratulations.

Dance-drama: Puck's speech (above) and the Fairy's second speech; full movement mime by one or more players. The speeches can be read by one reader or as a chorus; music can be used instead of the reading.

Other speeches as dance-drama: these can be performed in the same way after the details of hand-mime have been mastered.

LEARNING THE SPEECHES FOR PERFORMANCE
If all the preceding work has been done, one or more of

the speeches will have become very familiar through the reading and listening. Now they can be committed to memory with little extra effort. This will mean that the next stage in this work of entering this imaginative world can be tried.

Solo work

Using any of these four speeches which is known by heart, the player speaks the words while using his or her whole body, face and hands in full mime. The player is now completely in control of the sound, speed, rhythm, and the physical expression of these. It is an internal performance, satisfying the player's own standards.

Further pair work

The same work can be performed with a partner as:

1   audience: a silent observer who watches your attempt to communicate Shakespeare's poetic images through the various forms you use. Discussion can follow.

2   a deaf person. Your partner cannot hear your words, which you speak to guide your movements, but can see what you are saying through physical means. Discuss the effect afterwards.

3   a blind person. Your partner cannot see the mime which accompanies your spoken words, but will hear the effect that movement has on the way the words are spoken. In the discussion you may find that your partner was able to visualise your movements for particular images.

4   a mirror. There is no need to reverse all the movements as in a real mirror. Your partner follows your mime as closely as possible. Your partner may also speak the words, or take alternate lines or images, which may be several lines, or remain silent.

———•———

And thorough this distemperature we see
The seasons alter

II i second section: from *Enter Oberon, Titania* (l. 59)
to *Enter Demetrius, Helena* (l. 187)
OBERON · TITANIA · PUCK · FAIRY · ATTENDANTS

———•———

CONVERSATIONS FOR TWO

● An Elizabethan ploughman and his farm boy contemplate their fields of rotting green corn, their water-logged land, drowned sheep and diseased cattle. Never has there been such weather like it. There's been thick fog which has killed off many of the older people, wind, rain and sharp frosts. All this in summer! What can it mean?

● *As above for girls.* An Elizabethan farmer's wife and a visiting neighbour talk over the dreadful times they are living in. They recall wonderful summers when the fields were bursting with golden corn and their cattle were fat and healthy. Now everything and everyone seems to be dying off. They are faced with ruin and starvation.

● An Elizabethan townsman or townswoman visits a relative in the country. The countryman, or woman, lays all the blame for his ruined crops and dead animals on evil spirits and witchcraft. The townsman scoffs at these superstitions, pointing out that there has been bad weather everywhere, even in the town, and no one there really believes in magic any more. The countryman can tell him endless stories of bad luck, especially for those who scoff at the spirits.

● Titania and her votaress talk in the hot, scented air of an Indian night. The votaress gives Titania a small trifle:

perhaps some food or drink or a charm-bracelet. They laugh as they watch the big-bellied sails go by, especially as they remind them of the votaress's pregnancy. The votaress makes Titania promise that should anything happen to her she will take care of the child. She promises that nothing would ever make her give up caring for it.

● Two modern parents, now separated from one another, meet to discuss the custody of their child. The father insists that the mother hand the child over to him because he has the money to bring him up properly. The mother refuses because she cannot bear to part with the child, and because she can give the child her love. They cannot agree, and the quarrel drives them further apart.

● The father is in a pub with a friend, brooding over the fact that his wife, from whom he is separated, will not give him the custody of their son. Encouraged by his friend, the father grows more bitter and angry as he considers what he could give the child: a good home, and education and a good job; whereas, if he stays with his wife he'll have nothing and probably turn into a 'mother's boy'. He resolves to steal the child from her.

● *Boys or girls.* An old country gardener is showing his small grandchild around his garden. He tells him the names of the various flowers and herbs and how they can be used for making very potent wines, while others will heal burns or stings or ease rheumatism. He shows him the pansy, love-in-idleness, and tells the curious child how it came by its colour and how its juice was used.

Modern parallel

Oberon and Titania quarrel over the custody of the child given into Titania's care when the mother died in child-birth. The child may be Indian, possibly a prince. according to Puck; but Titania's story suggests that he simply happened to be born in India. Neither is the real parent; each spends much time travelling and they are often apart. If Titania hands the child to Oberon it is likely that she will see very little of him; he will be trained as a knight.

Although Shakespeare doesn't need to deal with this painful situation in depth, there is no doubt that there is a real quarrel between Oberon and Titania. Oberon's revenge becomes a cause for comedy, but it might easily have had a tragic outcome.

TITANIA as a wealthy, aristocratic woman who acts as foster-mother to the child.

OBERON as a Council Official who wants to place the child in a Children's home.

PUCK as a Welfare Worker who tries to get the foster-mother to see the official point of view.

THE CHILD need not appear. But see notes below.

Scenes: Oberon and Puck discuss Titania's application to adopt the child legally. They note that she and her husband travel a great deal, are often apart, and have many official and social duties to perform. She doesn't appear to be the ideal mother. Puck is sent to investigate.

Titania tells Puck the history of the child and shows that she loves him very dearly. If a child is cast, he could appear here. As said earlier, he is not necessarily Indian. He is clearly very fond of his foster-mother. Titania assures Puck that her travelling days are over and she will devote all her time to the child.

Puck reports back to Oberon who feels the child would have much more security and care in a Children's Home. He orders Puck to obtain the child. Puck is reluctant so they go together.

There is a fierce quarrel between Titania and Oberon with Puck trying to make both sides see reason. Finally they leave, Titania still refusing to part with the child.

Oberon begins to make official arrangements for the forcible removal of the child. Puck comes in with news of the mother's illness, possibly brought on by worry. For the good of the child, she is now prepared to give him up. Oberon and Puck go to collect him.

Point of concentration: this play should make clear the conflict between love and reason, a constant theme of *A Midsummer Night's Dream.* Discuss what you learn about Shakespeare's play through the performance of this one.

GROUP MIMES

Text *from* TITANIA These are the forgeries of jealousy
to TITANIA The seasons alter.

lines 81 to 107

This speech is packed with images of confusion and disorder, begun in the quarrels in the fairy kingdom and reflected in the common world of man. In performance this speech is often severely cut because it is dismissed as mere decoration. In reading the eye and mind can skip lightly over it. A personal exploration in terms of movement, music and the speech spoken will enable us to see the images afresh and the whole speech as vital to the poetic drama of the play.

SPEAKER (for Titania's speech)
TITANIA
OBERON } also as OLD PEOPLE and TRAVELLER
PLOUGHMAN also as FATHER
ELEMENTS (Wind, Fog, Water)
PLAYERS
CORN
ANIMALS, CROWS, CHILDREN } pairs

With a whole class cast more freely, using small groups for each of the elements, for the corn, animals, crows. Give Oberon and Titania two or more attendants, and cast minor parts, such as the Traveller, separately. There can also be more than one ploughman, with oxen, and other families. Titania's speech can be spoken as a Chorus by a number of players.

The seasons alter
PLOUGHMAN · CORN · CHILDREN · ANIMALS
Music begins, light and gay. The ploughman harnesses

44

his oxen to the plough and treads slowly up and down the new furrows. Behind him the corn begins to shoot up into the light. A group of children play beside a stream and then run in to eat a meal of hot soup and fresh bread. The cattle gather beside the stream, grazing contentedly.

OBERON · TITANIA
During the first six lines of the speech Titania and Oberon come in with their attendants from opposite directions, meet happily and lead a circular dance.

WIND · FOG
'But with thy brawls . . .' The music becomes harsh and discordant as Oberon quarrels with Titania over the possession of the child. The wind rises and grows to a fury, scattering the dancers, but leaving Oberon and Titania raging at one another. The wind draws up the fog (a group lying to one side) which spreads over the whole area, circling about the ploughman struggling home, beating at the green corn, separating the animals.

FAMILY · WATER
The people crouch and shiver and bend together for warmth and comfort; the animals herd together mournfully; the corn is gradually beaten down. Now the water rises and bursts over them all, swirling children and animals away and leaving the corn flat and ruined. Titania and Oberon hurry off.

CROWS · PLAYERS · TRAVELLER · OLD PEOPLE
The storm eases away, but the countryside is a picture of desolation. 'The ox hath therefore . . .' sees the ploughman brooding over his smashed crops and dying animals over which crows settle, feed and leave, barely able to fly. The 'nine men' players search in vain for their playing squares, while a traveller wanders lost in search of familiar landmarks and paths. The father comes into his house with wet wood which refuses to burn; the hungry children snatch at the few scraps of food they are offered; and the old people cough and choke with heavy chills.

Music: *Symphony No. 8* by Vagn Holboe (third movement), Turnabout TV34168S, or passages from *Scheherezade* or Beethoven's *Pastoral Symphony*.

Rich with merchandise
This mime is based on Titania's speech, 'Set your heart at rest...' lines 121 to 137. It is full of happiness and laughter with a contrasting sadness in the final lines. It can be played quite simply by two girls, but a third, speaking the lines, would help. There could also be other women— Titania's attendants—and others to represent the trading ships, perhaps with sailors loading and unloading and waving to the women. The birth of the child can be mimed directly or in a symbolic dance which creates the idea of birth and death generally, in nature as well as mankind.

Music: Stravinsky's *The Rite of Spring*.

Between the cold moon and earth
A series of mimes for pairs based on the text.
From OBERON Well, go thy way. Thou shalt not from this grove
to OBERON I'll make her render up her page to me.

lines 146 to 185

Puck says very little, and the work concentrates on the images in Oberon's three speeches.

Work on each speech separately at first, following the programme outlined below. After working on each, play through all three speeches as one unit.
1 *Listening.* Partner sits with eyes shut listening to the reading of Oberon's first speech, or either of the others. Do not try to visualise the images, but hear the words as if for the first time. Discuss and change over.
2 *Visualising.* Let the words call up personal images of singing, dolphins, the sea, stars and music. Discuss vivid images and where you found it difficult to 'see'. Change over parts.
3 *Hand-mime.* During a first slow reading use your hands as a physical language to express your idea of the images,

making them clear to yourself. Discuss and change over.

4 *Continuous movement*. Repeat the hand-mime working towards a continuous flow of movement from the expression of one image to another. During pauses or emphasis the position of the hands should not be altered. Because the performer is now in control, the reader must match his reading to the performance.

5 *The face*. Allow the face to assist the language of your hands. In Oberon's first speech it can reflect his anger which softens as he addresses Puck, his reverie as his mind slips back to recall the mermaid on the dolphin's back, and the strength and excitement of the 'rude sea' and of certain stars 'shot madly from their spheres'. This does not mean that the face has not been used previously, but that now it is a conscious part of the communication.

6 *Whole body*. Now this speech, and the others, can be tried using face and hands and whole body movement to express physically the rhythms of the verse and the images in it. This can be done with a reader or alone when the words are known by heart. (See notes on Solo work or with partner, page 40.)

TALKING ABOUT ACTING 4

A Master Magician

One usually assumes that the poetry of *A Midsummer Night's Dream* is a light, insubstantial thing, tripping gaily through a flimsy fairy-tale about the wedding of an improbable duke, the quarrels of tiresome young lovers lost in a wood, and the horseplay of Mechanics in well-meant but futile efforts to entertain. It is Mr Brook's great achievement, executed with supreme gravity and beauty by Mr Howard (in the double roles of Theseus and Oberon), and with sudden illuminations of happiness foreseen by John Kane's Puck, to have discovered that this is not so.

It is on the contrary, in its serenity, profound and thoughtful,

47

confident in its conviction that after many vicissitudes all will be well. Throughout the performance one feels that there is a Power, prone to blundering and often malicious, but which on the whole and finally leads to righteousness. Even in the working men, with David Waller earthy, good-natured, and impetuous as Bottom, there is a suggestion of the supernatural, for the frail, untroubled smile of Philip Locke's Quince is that of a man who has seen a vision not of this world.

The Power which Mr Brook suggestively, and without direct statement, creates through the delicate emphasis that Mr Howard and Mr Kane lay on certain passages in the verse, is not, like the Christian God, omnipotent and infallible. It is rich in errors, it frequently bungles the tasks it sets itself, and it is essentially a divided kingdom. On it however depends the well-being of humanity. So long as Oberon and Titania remain estranged, their inharmony will be reflected in the ordinary world of men and women, in which their attendants constantly interfere. This interference can be very frightening. The woods are coils of wire, and when the fairies swing these wildly through the air like venemous serpents to encircle Hermia the sense of evil and of danger in the theatre is very strong.

But there is never any doubt that eventually the evil will be overcome. It is at the points at which it assures us of this that Mr Kane's playful and mocking Puck is at its best. At the worst of his jealousy Mr Howard's Oberon is never deserted by a high seriousness that clearly sees the limits beyond which a humiliating and painful joke must not be pushed, either upon earth or in a world elsewhere. It is this that gives its great authority to his final speech, in which, when all the tumult and the shouting and the desperate distresses are over, Oberon lays on the house of Theseus and Hippolyta a solemn blessing. Mr Howard is right to take the speech slowly, as if every word had behind it the power of a god. It is the climax towards which the whole play has been moving. In it a god speaks, and a god should not be rushed.

HAROLD HOBSON reviewing Peter Brook's
1971 production at the Aldwych; *The Sunday Times*

Use me but as your spaniel: spurn me, strike me,
Neglect me, lose me; only give me leave,
Unworthy as I am, to follow you.

II i third section: from *Enter Demetrius, Helena* (l. 187) to end

OBERON · DEMETRIUS · HELENA · PUCK

CONVERSATIONS FOR TWO

● 'Your wrongs do set a scandal on my sex.' Two women discuss Helena's shameless behaviour in chasing after Demetrius. One knows about the Duke's decision that Hermia must marry Demetrius, the other has seen Helena in the wood. Is this the way a young lady should behave? What are young people coming to these days?

● Oberon tells Puck about the curious behaviour of the mortals where the women pursue the men, and the more they are insulted and rejected the more they love. Puck is foolish enough to think that the lovers' quarrels are very much like Oberon's quarrel with Titania—a great deal of fuss over very little. As a punishment, Oberon gives him a suitably difficult task.

● You are an ardent campaigner for Equal Rights for Women. Your friend prefers a more feminine and submissive role for women; she would much rather that things stayed as they were. To support her argument she tells you the story of Helena's unladylike pursuit of Demetrius in the wood. For you, this is a splendid example of Equal Rights.

● An elderly couple sit on a park bench observing the modern style of courting a girl. The husband notices how often it is the girl who does all the chasing while the boy pretends to be uninterested. It wasn't like that when they were courting. His wife is surprised at his innocence: did he really think he did all the chasing? A girl chases all right but, in her own way, without making it obvious.

HELENA AND DEMETRIUS: RELATIONSHIPS

I have loved her ever since I saw her; and still I see
  her beautiful.
If you love her, you cannot see her.
Why?
Because Love is blind.

The Two Gentlemen of Verona II i

'Why on earth can't she leave me alone? I don't want her —nobody does. Who does she think she is, chasing me around as if she was God's gift to men? Ugh! She makes me sick! I suppose it's flattering in a way—I mean, being so crazy about me, and after all I did like her once—once! There must be some way to get rid of her. I'm not having her mooning round me all the time. You'd think she'd have more respect for herself than that. She must be mad!'

Does Demetrius' thinking run along these lines, or is his attitude all part of the 'love game'? If his feelings and Helena's feelings towards him are genuine, then they are both in a very real and painful situation. He must hurt her to get rid of her while she must bear all the cutting things he says because she loves him.

WHAT HAPPENS IN PERFORMANCE?
Talking About Acting 5 and 6, pages 51, 52, show how this scene and the part of Helena are played as bright comedy. We can take the attitude that the more the lovers quarrel, and the more painful and desperate their situation is to them, the more we, the audience, will laugh. Or the scene might be played so realistically, with such a genuine concern for the painful emotions of this situation, that instead of laughing we are moved and sympathetically involved.

TALKING ABOUT ACTING 5

Peter Hall was content to direct the quartet (of lovers) to be young, foolish and clumsy . . . their verse is absurdly guyed, with exaggerated, unmusical stresses and with coarse tone and high pitch. Their actions are consistently clownish: for instance, as soon as Helena enters to Demetrius in the first woodland scene, she reaches towards him, misses, and collapses on the floor; before long, she is screaming and both are sitting on the floor, legs straight before them, on the other side of the stage. All four chase up and down the stairs (on either side on an 'inner' stage), lunge at each other, trip up, and spend much of the time on their backsides. When Lysander is charmed to love Helena and exclaims, with a show of reason, 'who will not change a raven for a dove?', he lays hold of Helena and pulls her round to face him, and soon Helena is lying on the stage with Lysander crouching close over her; his desire to read 'love's stories' in her eyes (which are for him 'love's richest book') and his attempts to 'honour Helen and to be her knight' lead only to horse-play, repetitive and crude.

The other fairies (apart from Titania) are like a pack of squabbling children . . . played consistently for a burlesque humour: the First Fairy announces that she has to 'hang a pearl in *every* cowslip's ear' as if she were some slut about to continue an endless and boring chore; and even when the fairies intend to dance 'solemnly' at Theseus' wedding, they arrive somersaulting and falling on the floor.

As well as ignoring the humanity and poetry of Shakespeare's comedy, Peter Hall also missed its width of appeal; it would seem that he pursued liveliness—or perhaps he would call it 'raciness' or 'burlesque'—too thoroughly; probably he was so bored with routine productions of this popular work that . . . he became too narrowly concerned with being brightly amusing.

J. R. BROWN reviewing Peter Hall's 1959 production
at Stratford-upon-Avon; *Shakespeare Survey 13*

TALKING ABOUT ACTING 6

━━━━●━━━━

But Helena, as Coral Browne played her, was almost the centre of the play. Ravishingly beautiful, utterly perplexed as to why Demetrius did not love her, anxiously trying with all her feather-weight mind to discover why Hermia should be happy while she was not, eagerly pursuing her love with plaintive squeals of 'Demeeeee . . . trius', she made a star part of a minor character. Her adventures in the wood were marvellously comic, her timing of each line, the value given to each grimace or expression, worthy of the most brilliant and sophisticated West End comedy. There were many happy touches; her discovery of the sleeping Lysander and the quick look over her shoulder for Hermia when he awoke and cried, 'And run through fire I will for thy sweet sake'; the injured vanity when she suspected that Lysander and Demetrius had ganged up to mock at her; the self-righteous appeal to Hermia's better nature; and finally the delicious complacency of a woman who is wooed by two handsome young men at once. The only thing that was wrong with this Helena was that the other three lovers were completely over-shadowed and became little more than 'feeds' . . .

MARY CLARKE reviewing Michael Benthall's 1957 production at the Old Vic; *Shakespeare at the Old Vic 5* Hamish Hamilton

━━━━●━━━━

THE LOVERS' QUARREL

Experiments with playing styles
Text: from Demetrius' entrance with Helena following him (l. 188) to their exits (l. 244).
Cast: only Demetrius and Helena, omitting Oberon, who watches the quarrel.
Improvise closely or freely in modern English.
After working on some of these playing styles, try to play the original text in one or more of them.

1   *As a modern romantic comedy.* Play this scene through as

modern teenagers using modern English. Although you play your parts seriously, you only touch on your feelings lightly. Your aim is to make the audience laugh.

2   *As broad, farcical comedy.* Look at the review (Talking About Acting 5) of Peter Hall's production. Use all kinds of exaggerated physical movement, such as is suggested in the review, to make the audience laugh; use the words simply as a means of moving from one situation to another; play words and movement at a fast pace. Work out exactly what you are going to do, try it slowly, then speed up.

3   *As a brilliant, sophisticated 'West End' comedy.* The two parts are played by young, fashionable stars, only concerned with their own scintillating performances. Look at the review (Talking About Acting 6) of Michael Benthall's production. Fill the lines with lightness and gaiety and the stage with busy (not farcical) movements, posturings and poutings. There isn't a thought or feeling in their bodies. The audience love every minute.

4   *As a personal experience.* Play the parts as if you were personally involved in this situation. You express your thoughts and feelings with complete conviction and sincerity; the audience may laugh, but for you it is quite serious. As Demetrius, you want to hurt; and you really are sick of her. As Helena, you are bitterly hurt, but you cannot stop loving. Forget any audience and play only to one another, hurting and being hurt.

5   *Experiments.* Play as a realistic drama of a middle-aged, married couple. Helena, the wife, is trying desperately to keep her husband who has fallen for another woman.

Play as a gentle comedy about two very elderly people. The frail and infirm movements contrast with their anger and passion. The old man, like Demetrius, is much more interested in another woman.

Play as a comedy of 'class' with Demetrius as a very rough labourer and Helena as a rich American widow hunting down her man. Demetrius is so afraid of being caught by her that he uses Hermia as an excuse to escape from her.

Play as melodrama, exaggerating movement and voice and working for great dramatic effect. Helena is the lily-white heroine, betrayed and discarded by the villain, who now seeks fresh conquests. When she pleads with him, it wrings your heart; when he threatens, it makes you gasp with fear.

THE ORIGINAL TEXT

This will be quite familiar after playing through several improvisations. Perhaps by cutting some of the speeches, learn this scene and play in some of the suggested styles.

DISCUSSION

Discuss: how playing in various styles helps you to see the relationships and the comedy; how some styles distort the original comedy and characterisation; how we need to see the play as a whole, keeping it in constant rehearsal in the 'theatre of the mind'.

Verbal drama

Oberon's speech:

> I know a bank where the wild thyme grows . . .
>   lines 249 to 267

The words are so familiar, so obviously beautiful as to create a barrier that results in mere acceptance. We need to progress beyond the meaning of the words and our appreciation of rhythm and texture to their enactment.

If we simply read the speech aloud we are in danger of making it sound, in Bernard Shaw's words, 'like insanely pompous prose'. (See his review, p. 55.) Unless we see the speech in the context of the play in performance, we ignore Shakespeare the dramatist. Then we can ask 'What is the effect?' instead of 'What is the meaning?'

The context of the speech
Looking at this part of the scene only, from Oberon:

> But who comes here? I am invisible,
> And I will overhear their conference.

what do we see?
> a passionate quarrel (Demetrius-Helena)
> an invisible observer
> the conflict unresolved
> a stormy exit (Demetrius)
> a tearful but determined exit, arousing our expectation: what will happen?
> Oberon's promise to help; we are assured that all will end happily
> a lively entrance (Puck)
> the exchange of the flower, arousing our expectation: how will it be used, what will happen?
> Oberon's speech, 'I know a bank . . .': the comedy to come is hinted at (see Group Play, page 56).

TALKING ABOUT ACTING 7

Powerful among the enemies of Shakespeare are the commentator and the elocutionist: the commentator because, not knowing Shakespeare's language, he sharpens his reasoning faculty . . . instead of sensitizing his artistic faculty to receive the impressions of moods and inflexions of feeling conveyed by word-music; the elocutionist because . . . he devotes his life to the art of breaking up verse in such a way as to make it sound like insanely pompous prose. The effect of this on Shakespeare's earlier verse, which is full of the naive delight of pure oscillation, to be enjoyed as an Italian enjoys a barcarolle, or a child a swing, or a baby a rocking-cradle, is destructively stupid.

BERNARD SHAW reviewing *All's Well that Ends Well*, 1895

GROUP PLAY

The Two Worlds
OBERON · PUCK · DEMETRIUS · HELENA
Improvise freely, beginning with Oberon:

> But who comes here? I am invisible . . .

to the end of this scene.

Your aim is to reveal the dramatic context of Oberon's 'I know a bank . . .' speech, which should be learned or closely improvised.

Pair work   Oberon's speech, 'I know a bank . . .'
The speech can be read in a variety of ways to a listening partner (Puck). Or it can be spoken directly if it has been learnt.

● From the beginning of Oberon's speech to 'And make her full of hateful fantasies.' Give this part as if Puck was not present, as your thoughts spoken aloud. Change your style and tone for the final part where you give Puck his orders. Partner should react only to this part.
● Speak the whole speech to Puck in a conspiratorial manner, plotting your revenge.
● You are a secret agent, giving instructions for the use of a deadly new drug to your No. 2. You know where to find your enemy, and you'll deal with her; your partner, if he takes care, can handle the other matter.
● Give the speech as 'insanely pompous prose', ignoring Puck as much as possible.
● Give the speech as an immensely dramatic reading, hinting at dark tragedy, a tale full of jealousy and hate.
● Give the speech as a beautiful fairy tale, telling it to a young, wide-eyed child (Puck).
● Give the speech as a gay Oberon enjoying the preparations of his joke and anticipating the comedy of Titania's 'hateful fantasies'.

Music: Benjamin Britten's opera *A Midsummer Night's Dream*. The familiar words 'I know a bank . . .' and other passages are revitalised by the singing and the score.

DISCUSSION
After performance, discuss the value of seeing a speech like this in its dramatic context. Look at the dramatist's use of contrast: between the noisy quarrel and Oberon's speech; between the discordant and abrupt dialogue of the mortals and the calm order and beauty of Oberon's world; between the angry movements and exits and Oberon's still and silent observation. Discuss the changes of mood and pace.

ACT TWO
Scene II

What thou seest when thou dost wake,
Do it for thy true love take

II ii first section: from *Enter Titania*
to *Enter Demetrius and Helena* (l. 89)

TITANIA · OBERON · PUCK · FIRST FAIRY ·
SECOND FAIRY · ATTENDANTS · LYSANDER · HERMIA

——————◆——————

CONVERSATIONS FOR TWO

● As Lysander and Hermia rest on their journey through the woods, she experiences some doubts and fears. Here she is alone with Lysander, and not yet married to him. What if he was unfaithful? How could she return to her parents? And how are they feeling now she has gone? Lysander earnestly reassures her.

● One fairy is instructed to 'stand sentinel' while Titania sleeps. If Oberon's cloak of invisibility was not effective with his fellow-fairies how did he succeed in passing him (or her)? In stage practice the sentinel is sometimes kidnapped by Oberon's attendants. He tells Titania what happened to him when she is released from the spell.

● The First and Second fairies discuss Titania's quarrel with Oberon. The First feels she ought to give up the child for the sake of the marriage and the happiness of the fairy kingdom. The Second thinks she should use her powers to spirit the child away so that Oberon cannot find him. Then they see Oberon with Titania, but they are too late to stop him. They try to rouse their mistress.

● Two young children see a present-day performance of this play and are totally enchanted with this fairy scene. As they talk about it, they go back-stage and see the set:

the artificial grass, the plywood trees, the spotlight moon, the fairies' costumes hanging up, the ass's head in a corner. Instead of disappointment, they see the magic of the stage which can create a fairy world out of these things.

● A scientist has discovered a powerful drug which he says will create universal happiness. There will be no more war or even quarrelling; everyone will love one another. Your advertising firm agrees to publicise the drug under the name of 'Flower Power'.

● You are desperately in love with a girl who does not love you. You are offered a drug, a love potion, which will cause her to fall in love with you. The offer is tempting, but you refuse.

GROUP PLAY:

Creating a New World
This is our second glimpse of the fairy world that Shakespeare creates; we get an impression of its fragility, its beauty and its size.

Science fiction attempts to describe the kind of life on Mars or Venus, of people like shimmering balls of light living in a world of pulsating energy. It recognises the possibility of a different, and perhaps higher, form of life.

Forget the bug-eyed monsters and create a beautiful, peaceful, different world in space, mainly through words and mime. Music will help. As in the fairy kingdom, there can also be other inhabitants which threaten the rulers. There is no real need to tell a complete story.

TALKING ABOUT ACTING 8

In a revival of the 1959 production of *A Midsummer Night's Dream*, the farcical performance of *Pyramus and Thisbe* and the Bergomask made the largest impression at the close. And elsewhere there was a marked tendency to choose one of several possible impressions and to work whole-heartedly for that: broad coltish humour in the lovers, an endearingly simple single-mindedness in the mechanicals, and verbal beauty in the fairies. This last attempt was a modification of the previous showing of this production, and entailed still moments when Titania, Oberon, or the First Fairy stood facing the audience, out of contact with other persons on the stage, to speak lines in a studied manner that was out of tone with the giggles, pouts and posturing of the rest of their fussy performances. Their speeches gave great delight, especially to the verbally conscious among the audience.

J. R. BROWN discussing the 1962 revival at Stratford-upon-Avon of Peter Hall's 1959 production; *Shakespeare's Plays in Performance*
Penguin

Verbal drama
Text: Titania's speech 'Come, now a roundel and a fairy song,' and the song, lines 1 to 32.
This scene can be explored using the techniques of hand-mime previously described:
> Listening
> Visualizing
> Basic hand-mime
> Continuous hand-mime
> The face
> The whole body

Pair work leading to group work: 1st pair: Titania's speech; 2nd pair: speeches of First and Second Fairy; 3rd pair: Chorus. The Fairy speeches could be split up for another pair, and Oberon's added.

WORKING METHOD
Pairs work on their part of the scene, using each of the six techniques above, beginning with 'listening'. Bring all the parts together to perform the whole scene which can include, if prepared, Oberon's speech.

Point of concentration: not only an impression of this tiny, beautiful, different world, but of the dangers that lurk within it.

———•———

The will of man is by his reason swayed,
And reason says you are the worthier maid.

II ii second section: from *Enter Demetrius and Helena* (l. 89) to end

DEMETRIUS · HELENA · LYSANDER · HERMIA

———•———

CONVERSATIONS FOR TWO

● 'I am as ugly as a bear'. Helena believes this is why Demetrius does not love her and she is utterly miserable. Her mother tries to find out why she is so miserable, and when she does, tries to give her back her confidence in herself and in her appearance through her own experience.

● You meet another girl you know slightly, but never say very much to. Suddenly, today, she comes up to you as if you were a long-lost friend, pleased to see you and anxious to know how you've been getting along. At first you make excuses to get away, but she clings to you. You become curious, so you stay. And you find out why she's so friendly.

● *Parts can be reversed for girls.* You meet a girl who is always running after a friend of yours although he doesn't like her. You decide to teach her a lesson by pretending that you like her. She knows you're making fun of her and is very hurt by it. You don't realise how cruel you're being and keep up the pretence.

● As Hermia awakes she sees Oberon disguised as a mortal. She tells him her dream of the snake eating her heart, and of the disappearance of Lysander. Oberon realises that Puck has made a mistake; this is spoken as Oberon's thoughts. He explains the dream, but assures her that she will get her Lysander back again.

● *Girls or boys.* You know that your friend and his girl are very fond of one another. Now he tells you that he's no longer interested in that girl, but in another he's scarcely noticed before. You can't believe this sudden change of heart, but he can find plenty of reasons for it.

The love game
Shakespeare's young people are in love one minute and hate the next, in an adolescent whirl of changing emotions. Like the youth of Verona in the play review on page 63, they are immediately recognisable as unaffected teenagers.

So Demetrius has fallen out of love with Helena and in love with Hermia. Hermia doesn't want him but it makes no difference; Demetrius doesn't want Helena but that makes no difference. Now, it seems, Lysander no longer loves Hermia; now Helena is everything to him.

Here is the irrational nature of love that Shakespeare portrays in the world of mortals, where, as Bottom says, 'reason and love keep little company together nowadays'. In *Romeo and Juliet* love is seen differently, as a stable and enduring passion that demands the whole self.

GROUP PLAY

Brief as the lightning

A game for four players: HELENA and HERMIA, LYSANDER and DEMETRIUS. Setting: modern.
This improvisation follows the pattern of the game in this part of the scene. It can be set in a park, on the beach, in a fairground. The happy lovers wander in, perhaps hot from walking in the sun or tired from swimming; they sit and rest, talk a little about the day, and Lysander dozes off. Hermia sees Demetrius hurry past and then Helena

looking for him. She waves to Helena who pretends not to see her. Hermia then falls asleep.

Demetrius and Helena return, quarrelling. He wants her to stop following him, she reminds him of his former love for her; he gives reasons for his change of heart but she will not listen. He runs off, leaving her hurt and bewildered. She thinks enviously of Hermia and feels acutely conscious of her ugliness.

She sees Hermia and decides to speak to her. At this moment Lysander wakes up and smiles at her. He asks why she looks so unhappy; he shows a sudden new affection for her, and suggests they leave Hermia while she's asleep. When she points out that he can't do that, for Hermia loves him, he tells her that that is all over. He thought he loved her but now he knows better. She thinks he is making fun of her and runs off in tears. He follows.

Hermia wakes up and looks round for Lysander. She searches and calls, growing increasingly upset. Then she remembers having seen Helena earlier on.

TALKING ABOUT ACTING 9

———————— ● ————————

. . . but all the youth of Verona were at ease. Running and sauntering, they were immediately recognisable as unaffected teenagers; they ate apples and threw them, splashed each other with water, mocked, laughed, shouted; they became serious, sulked, were puzzled; they misunderstood confidently and expressed affection freely. Much of this behaviour has been seen before in Peter Hall's production of *A Midsummer Night's Dream* . . .

. . . the stage-business seemed to spring from the words spoken, often lending them, in return, immediacy, zest or delicacy. So the unpompous behaviour caught the audience's interest for the characters and for the old story.

J. R. BROWN reviewing Franco Zeffirelli's 1960–62 production at the Old Vic; *Shakespeare's Plays in Performance* Penguin

———————— ● ————————

STAGE DESIGN

1

In the Old Vic production of 1953, 'confronted by a massively realistic wood, members of the audience began to peer about for live rabbits (such as Beerbohm Tree used in 1911).' In 1957 Michael Benthall went about things in a very different way.

The settings were all light and air. Against a pale landscape, in colours that suggested one of Claude's most luminous paintings, James Bailey (designer) placed a few elegant pillars for the Athenian scenes, and some trees, bushes and branches for the wood. There was nothing solid or substantial about these trees, however; they were almost transparent in the fragility. The costumes, too, for fairies and lovers, were sparkling, diaphanous, unreal. Only occasionally, with a fabric of warm, lustrous colour, would the paleness be relieved, and the design completed. The honest workmen of Athens were simply and soberly clad, in rough homespun or leather aprons. The costume for Oberon, dark green and irridescent, gave him the appearance of some strange, winged insect. . . .'

MARY CLARKE reviewing Michael Benthall's 1957 production at the Old Vic; *Shakespeare at the Old Vic 5* Hamish Hamilton

2

'. . . I once discussed with a friend how, if given our will, we would have *A Midsummer Night's Dream* presented. We agreed at length on this:

'The set scene should represent a large Elizabethan hall, panelled, having a lofty oak-timbered roof and an enormous staircase. The cavity under the staircase, occupying in breadth two-thirds of the stage, should be fronted with folding or sliding doors, which, being opened, should reveal the wood, recessed, moonlit, with its trees upon a flat arras or tapestry. On this secondary remoter stage the lovers should wander through their adventures, the fairies now conspiring in the quiet hall under the lantern, anon withdrawing into the woodland to befool the mortals straying their. Then, for the last scene and the interlude of *Pyramus and Thisbe*, the hall should be filled with lights and company. That over, the bridal couples go up the great staircase. Last of all—and after a long pause, when the house is quiet, the lantern all but extinguished, the hall looking vast and eerie, lit only by a last flicker from the hearth—the fairies, announced by Puck, should come tripping back, swarming forth from cupboards and down curtains, somersaulting downstairs, sliding down the baluster rails; all hushed as they fall to work with their brooms—hushed, save for one little voice and a thin, small chorus scarcely more audible than the last dropping embers:

> . . . Hand in hand, with fairy grace,
> Will we sing and bless this place.'

SIR ARTHUR QUILLER-COUCH, Shakespeare's Workmanship

3

His setting looked very much like an illustration of 'the Elizabethan Theatre' from one of the older text-books. It was constructed of unpainted wood, and, between two inward-turning stairways, it had an 'inner' and an 'upper' stage. For the woodland scenes, the painted backcloth depicting an Elizabethan interior was lit from behind so that it became transparent, and a grove of saplings was visible above the steps. The costumes were conservatively Elizabethan, some of them being copied from Hilliard miniatures.

J. R. BROWN reviewing Peter Hall's 1959 production
at Stratford-upon-Avon; Shakespeare Survey 13

4

A possible setting of the play in an Elizabethan playhouse. 'I believe that mediaeval and Elizabethan playwrights were just as vividly aware of the visual aspects of drama as any of their successors and took as much care to assist the spectator to an understanding of their plays through setting and costume as through verbal imagery; but they were careful, like the Greeks before them and unlike the Romans . . . to keep spectacle in a subordinate relationship to character and action.'

The actual scenic requirements of the play comprise three or possibly four simple and commonly used emblems: the throne (Theseus' palace), three or four trees (the wood), a mossy bank and possibly an arbour (for Titania). As all these scenic items formed part of the normal Revels Office stock, Court performance was readily provided for. In a public playhouse the throne would have been pre-set centre stage for Act I scene 1, to be taken up into the 'heavens' at the end of that scene and not to be lowered again until the start of Act V. The centre-stage area would thus have been free for the main action of the play within the wood. Each of the two stage doors (at rear stage) would in my opinion have been flanked and to some extent masked by a pair of trees: the alternating actions in different parts of the wood could then be easily represented by alternating use of the centre-stage/stage-left and centre-stage/stage-right areas. The locality of a highly mobile stage-action is thus constantly and easily identifiable for the spectator. The whole fore-stage is free at all times for action both before Theseus in the Palace and for the fairies, mechanicals and lovers in the wood.

> GLYNNE WICKHAM *Shakespeare's Dramatic Heritage*
> Routledge and Kegan Paul

5

The setting is a white box, ice-cold with purity, with galleries running along the top of the walls, and ladders to reach them at either side of the stage. Within the glaring whiteness of this symbolic chastity, emanating from the figure of the Virgin Queen, in all her meditation fancy-free, Mr Brook's players match the tricks of the circus—swinging from trapezes, spinning glittering plates on the ends of slender wands. . . . The woods are coils of wire, and when the fairies swing these wildly through the air like venemous serpents to encircle Hermia the sense of evil and of danger in the theatre is very strong.

> HAROLD HOBSON reviewing Peter Brook's 1971
> production at the Aldwych; *The Sunday Times*

STAGE DESIGN PROJECTS

There are five descriptions of stage settings for this play on the preceeding pages. They include brief notes on costumes. 1, 3 and 5 are actual production settings; 2 and 4 are suggestions, incorporating the writers' ideas of Elizabethan settings.

1 *Group*. Take one of the designs each, or between a pair, and by means of your argument, drawings and diagrams, perhaps on a blackboard, show how and why your design would be the most effective for performance.

2 Using a model of your own school stage or a typical proscenium stage, construct one of these setting designs to scale. If the set is attached to a separate base so that it can be removed from the model theatre, other designs can be shown in it.

3 *Group*. One half of the group to construct a model of Shakespeare's 'Globe' playhouse (see C. Walter Hodges, *The Globe Restored*, O.U.P.); the other half to construct one or both of the suggested Elizabethan sets: 2 and 4.

4 As a stage designer, prepare illustrations for any one of these settings, making a Ground Plan of the stage and set, based on your own stage if possible, with sketches of the whole set, scene changes, and particular details. You could also add working notes on materials, construction, size and colour.

5 As a stage designer, prepare illustrations for your own original settings for this play, using a Ground Plan and sketches as above.

6 Prepare sketches with notes on materials, size and colour for costumes for this play. It is not necessary to design each costume individually; for example, one for the fairies, one for the craftsmen, with suggestions for variations. Where possible, examples of material should be attached to the sketches. You must decide, first, which production you are designing for; it can be any of those given or for an original production.

7 Make a costume for one of the following: Oberon, Titania, Theseus, Hippolyta, Bottom or one of the lovers. This costume may be full-scale or doll- or puppet-size.

8 Demonstrate the uses of the Elizabethan stage on a

model using cut-out figures on rods. Dialogue can be added by reading it as the figures move. Select a scene, such as III ii or Act IV with a great deal of movement.

9 Choose one of the settings of the play's action, the wood or the Palace, and make scale models for it in a variety of styles: Elizabethan, any other period, realistic, highly imaginative and fanciful, abstract.

10 Visit to a professional production followed by a record of your impressions. You may decide to concentrate on a particular aspect of the production: lighting, costume, make-up, sets; or to deal with it in general terms.

Imaginative written work

In addition to writing play scripts for any of the Conversations, the following suggestions can be written by one or more pupils.

1 A description of the images visualized during work on a particular speech (which should be quoted or referred to). This kind of work is described on page 37.

2 A script for the Modern Parallel version of the Titania-Oberon quarrel over the changeling child on page 42. Split the work up amongst the players.

3 Write a modern commentary for any one of the Group Mimes; it can be designed for solo voice or chorus: *The Seasons Alter*, page 44, *Rich with Merchandise*, page 46, and *Between the Cold Moon and the Earth*, page 46.

4 Look at the reviews of productions in the Talking About Acting sections. Write a review of any two of the five Improvisations suggested on page 52. Decide whether your reviews will compare the two performances or deal with each quite separately.

5 Write a modern script for any of the Experiments suggested on page 53.

6 Write an imaginative script for *Creating a New World* which is described on page 59. This could also be prepared as a short story.

7 A script for the modern version of Shakespeare's love game: *Brief as the Lightning*, which is described on page 62. This is for four players.

8 Write a newspaper report on the marriage plans of Hermia, hinting at her disagreement with her father and mentioning the Duke's ruling on the matter. Provide a follow-up story with the news of her elopement with Lysander. Both stories can include interviews with the principals.

ACT THREE
Dream

OBERON . . . *When they next wake, all this derision*
Shall seem a dream and fruitless vision

ACT THREE
Scene I

Bless thee, Bottom! Bless thee! Thou art translated!

III i whole scene

BOTTOM · QUINCE · SNOUT · STARVELING · FLUTE ·
SNUG · PUCK · TITANIA · PEASEBLOSSOM · COBWEB · MOTH ·
MUSTARDSEED

———————● ———————

CONVERSATIONS FOR TWO

● Peaseblossom and Cobweb discuss Titania's sudden love for the transformed Bottom. Peaseblossom believes that the only explanation can be that this is Oberon's work: his revenge on her. Cobweb cannot think that Oberon would be so cruel. Why shouldn't she love an ass? After all, he is quite attractive, with those lovely long ears.

● Quince and Snout run into one another after seeing the transformed Bottom. Where is the Bottom they know and love? What did they see? As they get over their surprise and fright, Quince begins to suspect some silly joke of Bottom's: it's another example of his showing off, wanting to play every part. But Snout is certain it is magic, witchcraft. Their presence in the wood has offended the invisible powers.

● When Bottom goes into the 'tiring house' during the rehearsal Puck makes himself visible to him. Amazed and delighted, Bottom wants to call his friends; but Puck offers him a part in his play, and casts his spell. Bottom is unaware of any change in himself. Puck slowly disappears and Bottom goes to rejoin the actors.

● Before their rehearsal, another problem strikes the actors: when Thisbe kills himself there must be blood. Fearful Starveling is quite against this; like the killing itself, it should be left out. But Bottom, eager as ever to display his skill, can mix a dye to present blood, and they will say it is not blood.

● Bottom goes over his lines in the play (75 to 80) with his wife, who still thinks the whole enterprise is rather ridiculous and a waste of valuable time. When she hears the words and sees Bottom's performance she is convinced she is right. What a silly play! He explains the story to her, but she can only shake her head in disbelief.

● Two Elizabethan women discuss the play after seeing a performance at the Globe. The younger woman feels that no one would fall in love with someone who was ugly or disfigured by disease, no more than Titania would have loved an ass but for the juice of the flower. The older woman knows many women who love hideous men, and vice versa: you can't explain why. Love has this transforming power.

DRAMATIC METHOD

The play within the play

Any school pupil who has taken part in the school play will feel at home with this scene. He will have experienced some of the problems of producing a play: the construction of the set, the making of costumes and properties like the sword and the lion's mask, and the struggle with a difficult script (perhaps Shakespeare). But at the end, out of all the work and confusion you hope will come a play that will grip your audience's attention, whether it be through laughter, excitement or concern.

Right from this rehearsal the craftsmen's play is doomed to failure. It is not because they disagree, because this is done without bitterness or malice. Nor is it simply because they are not experienced actors, though the whole business of presenting a play is unfamiliar and uncomfortable to them. Is it the script? This is the story Shakespeare used for *Romeo and Juliet,* though the style, which he burleques, is strange and foreign to them.

The plain fact is that the craftsmen believe there is nothing more to the performance of a play than the putting on of costume and the speaking of the words. Rather than gain the audience's acceptance of the play—their 'willing suspension of disbelief'—they will begin by destroying dramatic illusion. So we must have the Prologue 'to say we will do no harm with our swords' and a lion that begs them 'not to fear, not to tremble'.

At every point imagination is dismissed. Practical men in a harsh world, to them the use and power of imagination is as unreal as the possibility of wealth and a long life. The Chorus appeals to the audience in *Henry V* to let the actor 'on your imaginary forces work'. Actor and audience must join in imaginative experience in order to bring the play to life.

Pair work : boys
● Bottom and Quince. Before the other actors arrive they discuss the practical problems of the play. Improvise this scene up to Puck's entry, using modern English in the present day. Quince raises all the problems which are brought up by others in the scene and Bottom tries to supply all the answers. Imagination has no part in their discussion.
● Quince and an imaginative producer. As above, they discuss the practical problems but here the producer is willing to rely on the imagination of his actors and the audience.
● Flute discuss the problems of playing Thisbe with Snug who is playing the lion. They go over Flute's lines, trying, and failing, to make anything of them. The words remain what Shakespeare intended: a parody. The lion experiments with a few lion-like movements and roarings that will not frighten the ladies, as well as his reminders to them that he is not a lion at all.
● Flute and an imaginative producer. As above, they discuss the problem of playing Thisbe convincingly. With

the producer's help Flute makes a serious attempt to understand his part and to find out how to say his lines in character. The producer might use some of the techniques, such as hand-mime, described earlier.

● The lion and an imaginative producer. The producer sees the lion as a vital and exciting moment in the play. He helps the actor to build up a picture of himself as a lion, in strength, colour, shape, movements, by advice and practical exercises.

In Peter Brook's 1971 production at the Aldwych, Snug's lion mask is 'a box, obviously made by the joiner himself in the likeness of a legless washstand with wooden whiskers'. (Ronald Bryden in *The Observer*.)

Pair work : girls

● An actress playing Titania (in the present day) discusses her part with a producer who is more concerned with the sets than with the imaginative life of the play. She plays her waking scene (learnt or improvised) up to line 134. The producer offers some off-hand suggestions which, when tried, only lead her to a more wooden and mechanical performance. But she needn't worry; the beautiful set will keep the audience interested.

● As above, an actress playing Titania discusses her part with an imaginative producer. They play through part of her waking scene, imagining the set and the other players. The producer reminds her of her rank as Queen, her transformation, and of the obvious visual comedy of this scene. They also see that the comedy lies in the contrast between the homely prose of Bottom and the beauty of word and rhythm of Titania's blank verse.

● Two girls are cast to play Puck, perhaps for different performances of the play. The first plays Puck as a comically rough and earth-bound goblin, enjoying his mischief and supernatural powers. The second misses all the fun in the movements and words and turns Puck into a sweet balletic fairy who speaks seriously to Bottom as if to punish him for his misdeeds.

PLAYING THESE SCENES

All these Pair Scenes can be played by either boys or girls or mixed pairs. Boys are frequently cast in female roles in school productions, and this will give a better understanding of character and scene.

Playing any of the mechanicals rehearsing his part means playing two parts at once: for example, Flute as a working man, and Flute playing Thisbe.

Shakespeare parodies the whole life of the theatre in this scene, and reveals the vital need for an imaginative response to the play; to mark this point, your playing should aim at an imaginative discussion of the play and an imaginative performance. Contrast this with a dull and mechanical performance. It is best if an imaginative and a contrasting performance are played, and perhaps shown, by the same pair.

Group work : After Pair work, aim to show two contrasting performances of the original scene, or of parts of it.

TALKING ABOUT ACTING 10

━━━━ ● ━━━━

. . . the actor who has no real grip of the character, but simply recites the speeches with a certain grace and intelligence, will be untrue. The more intent he is upon the words, and the less on the ideas that dictated them, the more likely he is to lay himself open to the charge of mechanical interpretation. It is perfectly possible to express to an audience all the involutions of thought, the speculation, doubt, wavering, which reveal the meditative but irresolute mind . . . In short, as we understand the people around us much better by personal intercourse than by all the revelations of written words—for *words*, as Tennyson says, '*half reveal and half conceal the soul within*'—so the drama has, on the whole, infinitely more suggestions when it is well acted than when it is interpreted by the unaided judgement of the student.

HENRY IRVING

━━━━ ● ━━━━

GROUP PLAYS

A Marvellous Convenient Place

Transform the craftsmen into modern factory workers with Quince as Foreman and Bottom as Leading Hand. They could also be a gang of builders, decorators, farmers, or fishermen. They are persuaded to prepare a play by the Mayor, or the Chairman, or a Union official, to celebrate a royal visit.

Though they doubt their abilities, they are ready to have a go, and Bottom's eagerness gives them encouragement; but the play itself presents more problems than they expected.

Pyramus and Thisbe needn't be used: find a play that offers some difficulty of language: a Restoration comedy with its artificial manners and elaborate style will work well. As in Shakespeare's rehearsal, only two or three speeches need be used.

The point of the play remains the same: only imagination will enable us to pass through the barrier of words to truth in performance. The workers' inadequate production forcibly reminds us of how to 'see' the rest of Shakespeare's play.

My Fair Lady

In Bernard Shaw's *Pygmalion* the flower girl is transformed into a lady; she learns how to speak properly and how to behave in society. In Shakespeare's transformation scene Bottom is the flower-girl, and like her tries to adapt himself to the high society of the Queen and her ladies-in-waiting, while the Queen herself is willing to 'educate' him:

> And I will purge thy mortal grossness so.

This scene can be played without the ass's head on Bottom; the point here is a difference of class, and Bottom's easy acceptance of all the riches, comforts and style of society life.

ACT THREE
Scene II

The sun was not so true unto the day
As he to me. Would he have stolen away
From sleeping Hermia?

III ii first section: from *Enter Oberon*
to *Puck: Lord, what fools these mortals be!* (l. 115).
OBERON · PUCK · DEMETRIUS · HERMIA

───────●───────

CONVERSATIONS FOR TWO

● Hermia, distressed, searches for Lysander and meets Helena, also distressed, looking for Demetrius. Hermia tells how she awoke and found Lysander missing. Helena is sympathetic, but she can't quite hide a feeling of being pleased with her friend's misfortune. Now she knows what it's like! Then Hermia wonders whether Demetrius has harmed her lover.

● Quince tells Bottom's wife what happened at their rehearsal, retelling Puck's story from his point of view, but she doesn't believe a word of it. Her husband missing! It's a joke, by him or them. But when he doesn't return she becomes alarmed. What have they done with him? What dreadful deed are they concealing?

● *Boys or girls*. Two friends work out a simple plan to get their own back on another boy or girl. They find a way to make a fool of him. One watches what happens and later tells his friend. He builds up his story, as Puck does, enjoying every moment of the telling and the success of the plan.

● A girl accuses a boy of spreading rumours about her to spoil her friendship with another boy. He hasn't been near her for days. What has happened to him?

78

What have you been telling him about her? Although you like the girl very much yourself, you certainly haven't done or said anything to the other boy. You try to say that you would never do anything to hurt her, but she doesn't believe you and storms off.

DRAMATIC METHOD

The incident described

Puck's speech, 'My mistress with a monster is in love', lines 6 to 34, describes action already seen. Why is it repeated in this way?

Shakespeare sometimes uses a character to describe action happening off-stage, that we do not see, particularly battles. It is not essential that we see Puck reporting the incident; Oberon could simply mention that Puck has told him about it.

What is the effect of this story-telling in performance? Through Puck's words we enjoy again the comedy of Bottom's translation, Titania's love, the craftsmen's fear, the resounding success of Puck's mischief. Our imaginations are worked on afresh to recall what we saw and what we felt then. If you like, a second helping of an attractive dish, a memorable tune in a concerto repeated but in a different time with different instruments.

What do we see now? Puck's enjoyment of the success of their scheme, his earthy sense of mischief: 'I led them on in this distracted fear'; and Oberon, listening.

THE ROLE OF THE LISTENER

Oberon must listen to 28 lines, perhaps one and a half minutes or so. How? Shakespeare, as thoughtful of his actors as of the audience, prepares him with Oberon's words before Puck appears.

OBERON I wonder if Titania be awaked;
          Then what it was that next came in her eye,
          Which she must dote on, in extremity.

His thoughts are all with Titania, his wife. There is still disagreement between them, and the unhappiness of the quarrel lingers. Will his plan restore their former happiness? What has happened? Where is Puck? Ah! here he comes at last: the eager greeting, the direct question. What has happened?:

> 'What night-rule now about this haunted grove?'

VARIATIONS
Pair work: boys/girls
In each of these variations the basic situation of Oberon waiting and Oberon listening to Puck's story remains the same. The variations occur in the manner of telling and the manner of listening. Some variations are only slightly different from what we might expect in a good performance; others are very different. Notes on playing, page 82.

Text: Oberon's speech, lines 1 to 5
Variation 1
Partner as audience to watch and discuss the effect with player afterwards. Oberon is full of good humour and eager expectation. The whole thing is a great joke.

Variation 2
Partner as audience, as above. Oberon is consumed with jealous thoughts of revenge. He only wants to be assured that Titania has been properly punished.

Variation 3
Partner as audience. Oberon speaks the lines as 'insanely pompous prose'. He is neither grave nor gay, eager or anxious. He simply says the words as beautifully as possible.

Variation 4
Partner as audience. Oberon is mildly curious and rather superior about his plan. Of course it will work out just as he planned, but it will be quite interesting to know what happened.

Variation 5
Partner as audience. Oberon is troubled and anxious.
Perhaps his plan will make matters worse. He becomes
irritable. Where is his servant? Is everything all right?

Variation.6
Partner as audience. Oberon is deep in thought. He
expresses concern rather than anxiety, but he can't help
a smile at the thought of her loving something strange. He
greets Puck with pleasure and eagerness, but there is a note
of anxiousness in his final question.

Playing: after performance and discussion, the part may
be repeated by the same player or the roles reversed.

Text: Puck's speech, lines 6 to 34.
Variation 1
Puck is afraid that his trick with the ass's head is not what
Oberon intended. He tells the story reluctantly and
nervously. Oberon is pleased with the first part of the story
and Puck grows confident; but when Oberon realises
that it is no monster at all, that his wife has been made a
fool of by Puck and a mortal, he becomes furious and Puck
is hardly able to finish. Oberon can interject brief comments like: What! How's this? and call Puck a fool.

Variation 2
Puck is bored with the whole affair. Must he go through it
all again? Why, he can hardly remember what happened.
He is urged on by Oberon's fearful threats and growing
irritation. All Oberon wants is to satisfy his desire for
revenge.

Variation 3
Puck tells the story with laughter and obvious relish; he
moves, mimes and embellishes the story with vivid
gesture. Oberon listens almost impassively, keenly following every word, his eyes bright, a smile slowly changing

his face; but physically he is a still centre surrounded by Puck's whirling action.

Variation 4
Puck tells the story at a mad, meaningless gallop like a nervous actor eager to remember all the words in a long speech. The speed kills all the fun and sense. The story is still important to Oberon, who tries to follow it with increasing desperation and annoyance. All his proper reactions of enjoyment and satisfaction are reduced to fleeting smiles and nods.

Playing: Oberon's short speech can be learnt or closely improvised. Puck's speech can be prepared this way or improvised freely in modern English. The player should make a framework of the main points of Puck's story.

This 'listening and telling' scene will demonstrate how much players depend on one another for a good performance. The effect of the story depends as much on Oberon's silent reactions as on Puck's telling of it. Wrong playing by either will distort Shakespeare's intentions. The audience can discuss what effect each variation makes on them.

If the scene is prepared in modern English, Oberon is free to interject brief remarks of his own to stress his reactions.

After presenting these variations, offer the audience (or for your own satisfaction) a valid performance in terms of listening and telling.

TALKING ABOUT ACTING 11

MICHEL SAINT-DENIS describes the actor's approach to his part, particularly in Shakespeare, and always remembering that we must consider the play as a whole as well as individual roles.

In a classical play the actor must not hurry or jump upon the character. You must not enslave the text by premature conception or feeling of the character. You should not hurry to get on the stage and try to act, physically and emotionally, too soon. Psychological and emotional understanding of a character should come through familiarity with the text, not from outside it. You must know how to wait, how to refuse, so as to remain free. You must be like a glove, open and flexible, but flat, and remaining flat at the beginning. Then by degrees the text, the imagination, the associations roused by the text penetrate you and bring you to life. Ways are prepared for the character to creep in slowly and animate the glove, the glove which is you, with your blood, with your nerves, with your breathing system, your voice, with the light of your own lucid control switching on and off. The whole complex machinery is at work; it has been put into action by the text. . . .

MICHEL SAINT-DENIS *Theatre: the Rediscovery of Style* Heinemann

---

DETAILED REHEARSAL

The Hermia-Demetrius quarrel
Text *from* PUCK I led them on in this distracted fear,
  to OBERON And laid the love juice on some true love's sight.

(lines 31 to 89)

This work deals with each of the three layers of comedy in turn:

> the reactions of Oberon and Puck to the mortals' quarrel–**Rehearsal 1**
> the seriousness of the quarrel to Hermia and Demetrius–**Rehearsal 2**
> the comic reversal of Demetrius' role–**Rehearsal 3**

All three Rehearsals are arranged for pair work, casting OBERON, PUCK/DEMETRIUS, HERMIA.

As Puck finishes telling the story of Titania to Oberon, Hermia and Demetrius come in quarrelling. We see a new pairing of the lovers and know, even more than Oberon,

83

what has happened; so we can laugh at the quarrel although it is quite serious and painful to them, and enjoy watching the effect of the quarrel on Oberon and Puck.

Performance will reveal how Shakespeare directs us to see the scene: how to enjoy the comedy of the situation rather than become involved in the pain of the relationship. Here, now, is poor Demetrius, hopelessly in love with Hermia, on the receiving end of the kind of treatment he gave Helena, who is hopelessly in love with him. Now, like her, he finds out how really painful rejected love is. He is abused and insulted and finally left, just as he left Helena. Comedy is ensured by this reversal, by the sight of Demetrius getting a taste of his own medicine.

1 **Rehearsal concentrating on the reactions of Puck and Oberon.**

Text: learn, improvise closely, or use modern English. Revision: Begin with the last four lines of Puck's speech, from line 31, and continue to 'And kill me too', line 49. Omit all the rest of the quarrel speeches. End with Oberon

> What hast thou done? Thou hast mistaken quite,
> And laid the love juice on some true love's sight.

Puck completes his story triumphantly. Oberon is delighted; and it seems his plans for the mortals are working out too. Then he sees the mortals coming.

> The aim here is to create a mood of merry mischief and successful planning. This contrasts sharply with the bitterness of the quarrel.

As soon as Puck sees the quarrelling pair he is puzzled. He has not seen Demetrius before, and he is not the man he worked the spell upon. Oberon reacts to Puck's 'This is the woman, but not this the man.' Demetrius' first words reveal Puck's mistake, and they both react.

> The aim is to show a reversal of mood: from mutual congratulations and happiness to feelings of anger and failure. As they have no words at this point, reactions must be conveyed facially and physically.

As the mortals quarrel, it is paralleled by the silent and invisible (to the mortals) quarrel between Oberon and Puck. The seven lines of the quarrel (43 to 49) are read by each player in turn, with the other reacting in character. After this the quarrel between Oberon and Puck can be developed without using the mortals' words so that the players can concentrate on reacting to one another.

Movement and expression should parallel the mortals' quarrel. This can be tried out now and developed when the mortals' quarrel is played by another pair. Oberon is strong and angry, like Hermia, and pursues and threatens Puck who, like Demetrius, retreats and protests. Oberon's words after the quarrel convey all the exasperation that has already been expressed silently: 'What hast thou done?'

2 Rehearsal concentrating on the seriousness of the quarrel to Hermia and Demetrius.

Text: learn, improvise closely, or use modern English. From their entrance to Demetrius' lying down to sleep.

The entrance, as always, is of vital importance. How do they come in? Together, or with Hermia first with Demetrius trailing after her, or vice versa? Is it a quick entry, by one, by both? When are their first words spoken? As they come in, when they are both on stage? Experiment to find the most effective entrance, one which tells the audience on sight about the relationship.

The aim here is to show the change of mood, from Oberon and Puck's merry happiness, physically, by the entrance itself. Right from the opening moments we should be able to see Demetrius' hopeless love for Hermia and her grief for Lysander.

At first Hermia is full of grief and despair; it is not yet a blazing row. The short line, 'And kill me too,' marks her feeling and suggests an action. What does she do?

Discuss and experiment. Her bewildered pain continues to: 'It cannot be but thou hast murdered him.' Now that she has an answer to Lysander's disappearance, she is hard and she looks coldly into Demetrius' face.

> The aim is to show Hermia's true love for Lysander and her growing hate for Demetrius. Demetrius is hurt by her grief and by her accusations.

His reply, 'So should the murdered look . . .' explains his expression, which she has mis-read, and he speaks gently to her. This soft speech rouses her anger. She advances on him, and then pleads again. This is her last weak moment; from now on she is made strong by her fury. The turning point of the quarrel is Demetrius' bitter-sad remark, 'I had rather give his carcass to my hounds.'

> The aim is to show the development of the quarrel and Hermia's growing strength. It is quite realistic and very serious; we can laugh at the situation, but they cannot.

Demetrius' reply cuts into her grief and whips her to a fury. She flies at him with biting sarcasm, and as she speaks of cowardice we see him forced to retreat before her. Now, as Helena said, the roles are reversed: 'When cowardice pursues, and valour flies' (II i.). It is this device of comic reversal that directs our laughter instead of our sympathy.

> Hermia's rage and scorn reach their height. It is not a mere slanging match; Hermia's deepest feelings are involved, and she wants to really hurt Demetrius. He is hurt, not only by her words, but because he loves her.

Demetrius does not return her insults. He simply pleads his innocence. She walks out on him with angry contempt and he is left feeling flat and exhausted.

> Hermia's exit is important here. It should remind us of Demetrius' exit, leaving Helena, in II.2. Does he just let her go without trying to stop her, or start after her and then give up? When does she say her last line: 'See me no more, whether he be dead or no'? Experiment with this exit.

3   Rehearsal concentrating on comic reversal

Text: the Demetrius-Helena quarrel from II i. From their entry (line 187) to their exits.

The situations in this scene, II i, are comically reversed in III ii. This 'reversal' is described in Rehearsal No. 2, the Demetrius-Hermia quarrel.

You can simply cast Demetrius and Helena for this rehearsal, or work on *both* scenes (this one and No. 2, the 'reversal' scene) by casting one player for Demetrius in both scenes and one player for Helena/Hermia.

These scenes can, of course, be cast separately for work by two pairs: II i—Demetrius, Helena; III ii—Demetrius, Hermia.

If the same pair work on *both* scenes (Rehearsals 2 and 3), they will find it easier and more interesting to mark the points for reversal in movement, gesture, expression and reaction. Players of this scene (Rehearsal 3) should read through the previous Rehearsal, No. 2, before starting.

The Demetrius-Helena quarrel from II i

Enter Demetrius, Helena following him. How the lovers come in is specified. Experiment here with the speed and manner of their entrance. Aim to suggest, visually, Demetrius' annoyance and Helena's love for him.

Compare this entry with the Demetrius-Hermia entry in III ii, (Rehearsal No. 2), by trying them out one after the other.

> Here we see Demetrius strong; in the reversal scene he is weak. He strikes out against the weak Helena. Hermia is strong in the reversal scene. Demetrius' dominance is shown in his movements, gestures and expressions as well as in the reactions of Helena.

'Do I entice you? . . .' As Demetrius insults and storms at Helena, she looks with the eyes of love and pleads gently to be allowed to remain near him. He tries threats: 'You do impeach your modesty too much . . .'. Her words say

87

that she is unafraid, but she might retreat in some alarm or remain stock still, though frightened. Experiment with her reactions to Demetrius' threats.

> In the reversal scene (III ii) Hermia's anger leads her to accuse Demetrius of cowardice: she flies at him and he retreats. Here, he threatens and Helena retreats protesting her love and innocence.

More threats: 'I'll run from thee . . .' Her alarm grows and she clings to him. Demetrius' sharp words, 'Let me go' give a clear direction to the action. He breaks free and starts off as she tearfully considers his treatment of her. When she looks up he is gone; she follows because she must, however much it hurts.

> Here is the reversal of role again. She suffers while Demetrius walks out on her.

Working in fours
Rehearsal 2: The Demetrius-Hermia quarrel:
OBERON · PUCK · DEMETRIUS · HERMIA
Refer to Rehearsal Notes, 1 and 2.
Rehearsal 3: The Demetrius-Helena quarrel:
OBERON · PUCK · DEMETRIUS · HELENA
Refer to Rehearsal Notes, 3.
Note: as Puck is not present during the Demetrius-Helena quarrel, begin the scene with Oberon instructing Puck to fetch the love-juice:

> Fetch me that flower—the herb I showed thee once.
> (line 169)

Play the quarrel, watched by Oberon with silent reactions, and end with Puck's return and Oberon's orders for the juice to be used on the Athenian. (II i, l. 245 to end.)
Performance: Present the two quarrel scenes, Demetrius, Hermia and Demetrius, Helena, to an audience. A narrator can explain the three layers of comedy (refer to page 83) and the comic effect achieved by the 'reversal'. The action can be stopped and replayed to make particular points.

Then will two at once woo one—
That must needs be sport alone

III ii second section: from *Oberon: Stand aside* (l. 116)
to *Exit Hermia* (l. 344)

OBERON · PUCK · DEMETRIUS · HERMIA · LYSANDER · HELENA

CONVERSATIONS FOR TWO

● Oberon and Puck comment on the lovers' quarrels as
they watch. Puck enjoys the behaviour of the foolish
mortals enormously; Oberon's amusement is more
dignified and detached, but every now and then he
reminds Puck that this is all his doing. Towards the end,
when a fight is threatened, Oberon becomes more and
more angry with Puck.
Playing: this conversation can be based on what each
player remembers of this scene, but various points for your
comments could be marked in the text of the play. For
performance, using six players, these marked points would
show the lovers when to pause to allow room for the
improvised dialogue of Puck and Oberon.
● Puck meets Titania after the night's events. He tells her
of the confusions of the lovers which his mischief caused.
She tells him of her strange love for an ass with a mixture
of embarrassment, relief, amusement and loathing. Puck
wisely does not laugh too much or reveal his part in the
affair; he is happy that she and Oberon are reunited.
Titania laughs at the mortals' 'fond pageant', contrasting
it with the harmony of the fairy kingdom.
● 'My legs are longer, though, to run away!' As Helena
makes her way back to Athens after her quarrel with
Hermia, she meets a spinster aunt. When she tells her

story—how two men love her at once—her aunt thinks it's marvellous! She should make the most of her opportunity, and not miss her chances as she did herself. As Helena listens to her aunt's sad stories she resolves to take the men at their word, and to catch Demetrius while she has the chance!

● After this scene, Hermia meets her father, Egeus, who is searching for her in the wood. He is furious with her for running away, disobeying both him and the Duke! She tells him how she has been betrayed by Lysander, how he is now chasing after Helena. Egeus has no sympathy for her. If she'd done as she was told. . . . Now she has been dishonoured by spending the night in the wood with Lysander, he will make him marry her whether he likes it or not. Though Hermia still loves him, this is the last thing she wants to happen.

● After this scene, and before his fight with Lysander, Demetrius tells a friend about the night's adventures. He is full of scorn and bitterness for Lysander, who now wants his girl. He feels that Lysander is deliberately annoying him: when he wanted Hermia, Lysander carried her off; now that he loves Helena, Lysander wants her. The friend agrees that Lysander can't be trusted and ought to be taught a sharp lesson. He goes off with Demetrius to watch the fight.

DRAMATIC METHOD

Climax

In the wood, as in a dream, everything changes:

> Or in the night, imagining some fear,
> How easy is a bush supposed a bear?

Titania, Bottom and the four lovers are all affected. In this scene the confusions of the night reach their comic climax, and are followed by a similar climax of the events in the fairy kingdom.

The diagrams on p. 94 show how Shakespeare has

prepared us for the climax by the reversal of the relationships. In a key speech, Titania drew a picture of how 'the seasons alter' (II i) : the natural order of things is disturbed by the disorder in the fairy kingdom. This image of confusion and disorder is reflected in the topsy-turvy affections of the mortals. When the comic confusions of the two worlds are at their height, Oberon will quickly restore the natural order.

For performance, each player must be aware of his or her relationship to each of the others: what he seeks now, what he sought formerly, what he rejects. This scene is composed of contesting forces of emotion, love and hate, wanting and being rejected, giving hurt and being hurt. In this battle no one wins, though for each one success is of paramount importance. In the end only confusion is triumphant; resolution and happiness must wait for Oberon and the next Act.

GROUP INTERVIEW

The characters engage in a painful struggle for love. What are their hopes, their fears now? What do they want? The interview examines identity and motive. Who are you? What do you want?

Each of the lovers is interviewed in turn by a panel of the other three. The questions can concern any aspect of the character's life including things which may have happened before the play began. If a question has no meaning for the character, he shoud simply say, 'I don't know.' All questions must be answered honestly and directly with no camouflage. Questioning should follow this pattern:

What is your name?

How old are you?

Where do you live?

Have you any rank or employment?

This may lead to other questions about his work, his master, and the people he works with.

What are your interests?
Who is your best friend?
Have you any enemies?
Further questions will find out why he likes or dislikes these people, how and when they meet, and what occurs.
How do you get on with your parents?
How do you get on with people in authority?
Are you happy and contented with your present life?
What do you want most of all?
What do you fear most of all?
Are you loyal to your friends?
Have you ever been disloyal to anyone?
Have you ever changed your mind about a person?
These questions, and particularly the last, should be answered as if this scene (III ii) had just occurred. Lysander, for example, will say that he used to love Hermia, but now he loves Helena.
What recent event most affected you? Hurt you? Pleased you?
What do you think is likely to happen to you in the future?

OBJECTIVES

What do you, as a character in this scene, fear, hope, want, like, dislike? All these feelings and motives are expressed in the speeches but they are often overlooked in the reading or not sufficiently explored in performance.

If you use these key words (fear, hope, want, like, dislike) in a short modern version of this scene, Shakespeare's language will seem less of a barrier.

Here is an example:

Enter Lysander and Helena

LYSANDER   I want you to believe me. I love you.

HELENA   You want to make fun of me. You love Hermia.

LYSANDER   I didn't know what I was doing then.

HELENA	You don't now if you give her up.
LYSANDER	Demetrius is in love with *her* now, not you.
DEMETRIUS	(*waking*) Helen, I love you!
HELENA	You both want to make fun of me. You both hate me, and you both love Hermia. Now you want to hurt me.
LYSANDER	You love Hermia, Demetrius, and you can have her. I love Helena.
HELENA	You're wasting your time making fun of me.
DEMETRIUS	You keep Hermia, Lysander. You love her. I don't want her now. I love Helena as I used to.
LYSANDER	I don't love Hermia, Helena. I love you.
DEMETRIUS	You do not love her. Here comes your love —Hermia.
HERMIA	I want to know why you left me, Lysander.
LYSANDER	Why should I want to stay with you? I wanted to follow my new love.
HERMIA	What new love? You love me.
LYSANDER	I hate you. I don't want you following me. I love Helena.
HERMIA	You can't mean that. You're hurting me, making fun of me. I know you love me.
HELENA	She wants to make fun of me as well!—Why do you want to hurt me, your closest friend?
HERMIA	I don't want to hurt you or make fun of you. I think you want to hurt me.
HELENA	You've made Lysander pretend he loves me and you've made your other love, Demetrius—who hates me—praise me. If he hates me, why does he say he loves me? And Lysander would only do what you want him to do. How can you hurt me like this?
HERMIA	I haven't done anything. I don't want to hurt you.

HELENA Go on pretending! You all want to hurt me just for the fun of it! I'm not staying to listen to it.

LYSANDER Don't go, Helena: I love you!

REVERSAL OF RELATIONSHIPS

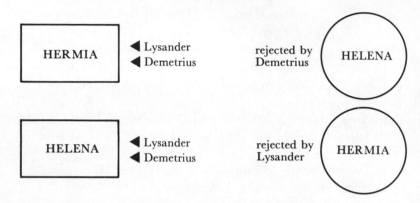

CHANGING PATTERN OF RELATIONSHIP

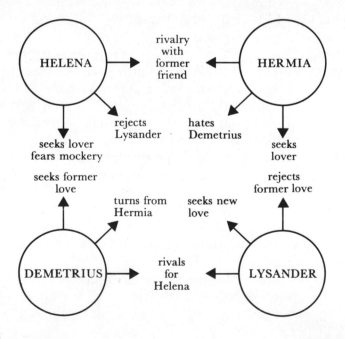

PLAYING THE SCENE

Use the script as a second step, after the Interview, in working towards a closely improvised or learnt version of the original scene.

In performance, keep your own objectives clearly before you; you should know exactly how you feel towards each of the other characters, and how each feels towards you. The aim is to make these feelings explicit, to yourselves and to any audience.

GROUP PLAY

The Course of True Love
HELENA · HERMIA · DEMETRIUS · LYSANDER

Play in a completely modern style as young people of your own age or slightly older. Use your own names instead of the characters' names. Choose a realistic setting.

This improvisation follows the structure of this scene. You are trying to reveal the structure and the pattern of relationships in a very free and imaginative play which appears to be completely new and modern.

1 Lysander declares his love for Helena; she rejects him.

2 Demetrius declares his love for Helena; she thinks they are making fun of her.

3 Hermia is puzzled and upset by Lysander's rejection of her.

4 Helena attacks Hermia for conspiring with the men and encouraging them to mock her.

5 The men's rivalry over Helena becomes bitter and angry. Lysander firmly rejects Hermia, who realises that he really is in love with Helena.

6 Hermia attacks Helena for stealing her love away. Helena asks the men to protect her from Hermia. She tries to patch up the quarrel.

7 The men quarrel over who shall protect Helena. They go off to fight. Hermia blames Helena for all this trouble and Helena runs away.

VARIATIONS
Give the characters a different nationality or give them
markedly different accents and manners.
   Set in an unlikely scene: a factory, on a boating lake, in
a library, at a Youth Club, at a party, perhaps where
masks are used, at a dance, at a fairground. Several places
could be used.

———•———

   Like to Lysander sometime frame thy tongue,
   Then stir Demetrius up with bitter wrong

III ii third section: from *Oberon and Puck come
forward* (l. 345) to end

OBERON · PUCK · DEMETRIUS · LYSANDER · HELENA · HERMIA

———•———

CONVERSATIONS FOR TWO

● Puck tells Oberon about his latest mischief: the fooling
of the two men in the wood. Like his story of Bottom and
Titania, he conveys all the fun of the event and his delight
in the telling. Before Oberon praises him, he carefully
questions Puck about using the herb on Lysander. Has he
got it right this time?
● Two Elizabethans (husband and wife, two men or two
women) pass through the wood on their way to work. They
hear the noise of the two men crashing about searching
for one another. They hear other voices, something like
human voices, but not quite. The wood is bewitched!
● As Hermia lies down to sleep, Puck appears before her.
He tells her not to worry about Lysander, he will not be
harmed, and in the morning he will love her again. She is
too exhausted to argue and thinks she must be dreaming.

Foolishly he tells her that he made Lysander fall in love with Helena—a mistake, of course, but good fun.

● As Helena falls into a troubled sleep, Puck speaks to her without waking her. All shall be well. When you wake Demetrius will truly love you and you will be happy again. No, she can't believe this; she has been hurt too often, by too many people. He used to love her, he says he loves her now, but he's only making fun of her. Puck repeats his promise until she begins to think it is possible, until she believes all he says, and falls into a contented sleep.

VISUAL COMEDY

Comedy of voices and darkness
After the excitement and comedy of the verbal battle between the lovers comes comedy of action.

> Off go the men: line 338
> Off go the women: lines 343, 344
> Puck and Oberon come forward: line 345
> Oberon exits: line 395
> Lysander enters: line 401
> and exits: line 404
> Demetrius enters: line 404
> and exits with Puck: line 412
> Lysander returns: line 413
> and sleeps: line 420
> Puck and Demetrius enter: line 420
> Demetrius sleeps: line 430
> Helena enters and sleeps: line 436
> Hermia enters and sleeps: line 447

The rapid entrances and exits sweep the play from verbal comedy to physical comedy. Then, as each weary lover falls asleep, the pace slows step by step until the scene is quiet and still, and 'all shall be well.'

The playing of this scene is vital to its comic life. Just how movement enhances the verbal comedy must be seen and experienced by the player. Shakespeare is writing visual comedy, which needs physical expression: we laugh at what happens, what is done rather than at what is said.

Puck's 'voices' contribute to the comedy and are the mainspring that keeps the physical comedy going. With Puck in command, the men can never meet, the quarrel can never end in disaster: we are directed towards comedy not tragedy. And Oberon has already told us, speaking to Puck before the chase, that when the men are tired Lysander will be given remedy and 'all things shall be at peace'.

GROUP PLAY

Bragging to the Stars
A comedy of movement for six players
OBERON · PUCK · HELENA · HERMIA · LYSANDER · DEMETRIUS
From line 335, 'Now she holds me not.' to the end.
Mark out two rear entrances and two side entrances left and right.

PLAYING METHOD
Follow the outline of entrances and exits given on p. 97. Improvise your dialogue freely, concentrating on the movement. Your first rehearsal should be a 'walk-through', simply getting the feel of each entrance and exit. Follow this by stepping up the speed of movement; a third rehearsal should give you the pace you require.

Puck should make some attempt to imitate the voices, but should concentrate on movement.

Movement is affected by the fact that it is night and they are in a wood. For the men this means that one may be ambushed by the other or one may come upon the other unexpectedly. Danger lurks in every bush. Anger and frustration drives them to a wild, eager search of every corner.

For the women the night and the wood mean loneliness, weariness and torn dresses. While the men leap and bound with the fierce energy of battle, the women walk slowly and painfully, foot-sore and torn by briars, drooping from unhappiness.

In this improvisation, Oberon can remain on stage to watch the comedy and perhaps to comment.

VARIATIONS

Night: this, of course, can be suggested both by the playing and by the use of a moon-lit stage. Try playing this scene under very bright white light with the actors behaving as though they were in complete darkness. This effect will not be achieved by playing in ordinary day-light; it must be on a stage or an area where lighting effects are possible. The stage should also be completely bare; the actors, again, imagine all the trees and obstacles in their playing.

Set: transform this exterior set into an interior: the typical lounge or bedroom of the French farce. Fill it with appropriate furniture, cupboards, four doors and perhaps a window with a balcony. The men will search behind chairs and in cupboards and look into various rooms. The women fall asleep in the chairs or on the bed. The light switch, needless to say, doesn't work.

Puck's voices: if Lysander and Demetrius each uses a very different speaking voice from his normal one, it will make it easier and more effective for Puck's imitations. Strong dialect can be used or foreign accents or 'class' accents, perhaps contrasting working class with upper class.

Original scene: after these improvisations, a closely improvised or learnt version of the scene can be attempted.

Pace: variations in the pace of playing can be tried, from slow to fast and too fast. An interesting variation can be made by playing the scene at the correct pace but slowing down each player's movements as he or she comes in and sleeps. These movements can assume a dream-like quality rather like a film in slow-motion. Use the final speeches of each player to gradually reduce speed until the lying down itself is in slow-motion.

VERBAL DRAMA

Change of mood

Text *from* OBERON This is thy negligence. Still thou mistakest, *to* OBERON We may effect this business yet ere day.

lines 345 to 395

Between the verbal comedy and the physical comedy there is a short quiet period when Oberon makes plans to restore the natural order which must be effected before day-break.

Dramatically this is important because it puts Oberon in control again, reminds us of the comic intention, and provides a rest and contrast from laughter before the fast and furious coda of the chase.

Pair work: Puck's speech, lines 378 to 387 and Oberon's speech, lines 388 to 395.

● Select a piece of intrumental music which is fast and vigorous, suggesting the lovers' quarrel. Play part of this, fade out or down, and speak the two speeches. Complete with music to suggest the chase.

You may find a piece of music which has a quiet passage set between two lively passages. Look at the final movements of well-known symphonies.

● Use the Mime work described on pages 36–40, starting with Listening and Visualising.

● *Variations:* speak Puck's speech with a country accent, giving expression to all the fear and horrors of ghosts and graves.

● Speak Oberon's speech in a dream-like whisper, softly, gently, slowly. Increase pace and volume slightly in the final two lines.

● Speak Puck's speech with whispered, anxious excitement. Puck is afraid of these other 'damnèd spirits'.

● Speak Oberon's speech with a gracious air of superiority; a rather pompous king very satisfied with his power.

Imaginative written work

In addition to writing a script for any of the Conversations in this Act, the following can be written by one or more pupils.

● Pair work on the craftsmen's rehearsal of their play is suggested on pages 74, 75. Write an account of your Pair rehearsal either as Rehearsal Notes or as a play script.

● Write a play review of two contrasting performances, an imaginative one and a mechanical one, of III i. This is suggested after Pair work on page 76.

● A script for a modern play, *A Marvellous Convenient Place* which is described on page 77. This can include extracts from *Pyramus and Thisbe* or from a play especially written for the craftsmen. (See below.)

● Write your own *Pyramus and Thisbe* play for a group of modern workers. This should be as difficult and clumsy as you can make it, but the story should be very simple. You can base your play on another (but not Shakespeare), parodying the style and exaggerating the incidents.

● A Group Play, *My Fair Lady*, is suggested on page 77. Write a script for this after improvising it. The play can be written for a pair or a group.

● As a series of short play reviews, discuss the effect of the Variations on either Oberon's speech or Puck's speech which are suggested on pages 80–82.

● Watch several rehearsals of any of the three suggested rehearsals of the Hermia-Demetrius quarrel which is described on pages 83–88, and write a play review of the result or a Rehearsal Diary showing the players' progress.

● An *Objectives* scene is described, with an example of writing, on pages 92–94. Complete this script by working from the original text and from your discussions in rehearsal.

● *The Course of True Love* on page 95 suggests using the basic structure of the scene for a modern version of the sudden loves and hates of adolescents. Write a script based on your improvisation of this, or an account of how it contributed to your understanding of Shakespeare.

● Write a script for the movement play, *Bragging to the*

Stars, which is described on page 98.

● Look at the play reviews in this book and discuss the merits and defects which receive comment. From your experience of reading, watching and rehearsing, add your own comments on these productions.

● Look at the comments on the art of acting in this book. Take up any points which you find particularly interesting or revealing and, from your rehearsal experience, add your own comments.

ACT FOUR
Waking

BOTTOM ... *I have had a most rare vision. I have had a dream past the wit of man to say what dream it was.*

ACT FOUR
Scenes I and II

My Oberon, what visions have I seen!
Methought I was enamoured of an ass.

IV i first section: from *Enter Titania, Bottom and Fairies*
to *Exeunt Oberon, Titania and Puck* (l. 101)

TITANIA · BOTTOM · 4 FAIRIES · OBERON · PUCK

———————●———————

CONVERSATIONS FOR TWO

- 'How came these things to pass?' Titania sees the ass she
loved and the four lovers asleep. She makes Oberon tell
her what has happened. She soon discovers that Oberon
used his powers on her, that his servant, Puck, caused the
lovers to quarrel, and that she has given up the changeling
child while still under the spell.
- Bottom tells Titania about his old life, when, it seems,
he was a craftsman in Athens. He has faint memories of
his friends, and of a play. Titania promises him a wonderful new life with her where his every wish will be obeyed.
Bottom agrees that this life is very different, but he misses
working with his hands; and she suggests some suitable
work.
- Cobweb and Peaseblossom discuss Titania's meeting
with Oberon when she gave him the child. Peaseblossom
is certain that Titania is under some spell, otherwise she
would never be in love with an ass and never have parted
with the child. Cobweb thinks Titania has been very
sensible: the child is growing up and she was anxious to
end the quarrel with her husband. But they are becoming
tired of running errands for Bottom.
- A performance of this play is taking place at The Globe.

A curtain has been drawn across the alcove at the rear of the stage. This conceals Bottom, after Puck has removed his head, from Theseus and the others when they come in. While he waits for his next appearance, Bottom talks to the prompter about how the audience is receiving the play, and especially the comedy. The ass's head has made Bottom hot and tired, and the sun is beating down, too; worst of all, the silly boys playing the fairies are getting more laughs and applause than he is.

MISSING SCENE

> For, meeting her of late behind the wood
> Seeking sweet favours for this hateful fool,
> I did upbraid her and fall out with her

OBERON · TITANIA · BOTTOM · FAIRIES

Oberon describes in detail his meeting with Titania and Bottom, who is now garlanded with flowers. The joke seems to have turned a little sour because of Titania's love for 'this hateful fool'. He is angry and jealous; he laughs at her foolishness, until she willingly gives him the changeling child. A fairy is ordered to take the child to Oberon's bower. Text: IV i, lines 45 to 60.

The scene opens with Titania showing Bottom the fairy wonders of her kingdom. Bottom, as in the second Conversation, compares his old life to his new, while the fairies collect the flowers for his garland. Oberon watches for a while until he bursts upon them angrily.

The scene can continue as outlined above, or Oberon can tell her that her love is a dream caused by Cupid's flower; he will release her if she gives him the child. If she is reluctant, or doesn't believe him, Oberon can threaten to use his powers to take away her lover.

A Most Rare Vision
The missing scene can be followed immediately with a learnt or improvised version of this present scene ending

with the dance. And, of course, all the scenes between Oberon and Titania can be put together as one play, *A Most Rare Vision*. For this version, the craftsmen's rehearsal could be omitted and Bottom introduced after his transformation. All reference to the lovers would also be omitted.

TALKING ABOUT ACTING 12

———●———

JOHN KANE who played Puck in Peter Brook's 1970 production of the play describes his experience in rehearsal.

A very brief exploration of the text reveals three very different worlds in *A Midsummer Night's Dream*, the Mechanicals, the Lovers and the Spirit World of Theseus/Oberon, Hippolyta/Titania. During rehearsals, a fourth world emerged. We decided that if Spirits were omnipresent it would be impossible for them to be confined to the 'Fairy' scenes. They must be available to speak the lines of Titania's fairies, but they could also be around to lower trees for the Lovers, carry lumber for the Mechanicals and produce sound effects wherever appropriate. The actress and three actors playing Spirits were dubbed 'Audio-Visuals' and were given complete licence in the early days.

With the setting of the Mechanicals' scene these Audio-Visuals made a first appearance; from there on the run-through assumed a different character. Most of the company still had their books in their hands which obviously hampered them, but not the AVs. They were free to wander where they pleased and assist or screw-up whatever they liked. It soon became obvious that the Spirits that morning were certainly mischievous if not downright malevolent. The forest and its inhabitants exuded a primitive savagery that infected everyone who came into contact with them. As the group feeling grew, a wild gaiety seized the company. With books in one hand and a hoop or a cushion in the other, we whipped the play along like some frantic bobbing top until it eventually exploded during the Titania/Bottom confrontation in a welter of torn newspaper, cardboard phalluses and Felix Mendelssohn.

As the noise and the laughter died away, we looked around the room and as though awakening from a dream ourselves we realised that we had been possessed by some wild anarchic force, that we had been in contact with elements of the play that no amount of discussion or carefully plotted 'production' could have revealed.

JOHN KANE interviewed in *The Sunday Times*

Visual impact

Much of the comedy of this scene can be realised in a reading and it can hardly fail to be funny in a classroom performance. This scene, and Bottom's first scene with Titania (III i), are full of opportunities for visual comedy.

What we lose is the fresh impact of the grotesque head, the splendidly-robed figure of the proud Queen in love with a poor craftsman, the busy attendance of the fairies. Unlike the Elizabethan audience, we have read the play before seeing it or acting it. We may be surprised to find Shakespeare still funny in performance, but we are not surprised—startled into laughter—by Bottom's appearance and Titania's devotion.

If we imagine the first rehearsals of the new play at The Globe . . .
'As for the actors, as I noticed in England, they are given instruction daily as if at school; even the leading actors expect to take instruction from the playwrights.'

(Johannes Rhenanus, writing in 1613.)

A FIRST PERFORMANCE

SHAKESPEARE · KEMPE · BURBAGE · BOYS FOR
TITANIA AND 3 OR 4 FAIRIES
Shakespeare is telling the story of his new play to the actors of the Lord Chamberlain's Company on the stage of their new theatre. As a member of the company Shakespeare has cast himself as Peter Quince, William Kempe the

comedian as Bottom, and Richard Burbage as Oberon. Kempe asks whether the scenes with the ass's head will really work. The boy playing Titania is not sure how to show a Queen in love with something so foolish. Shakespeare reminds them that it must be their imagination which will create the comedy and induce the imagination of the audience to accept it.

He decides to rehearse just this scene (lines 1 to 44). In fact it will help him to write it, and he will be pleas∶d to use any suggestions. He outlines the scene to Titania, Bottom and the four fairies and calls for the ass's head.

As soon as Kempe puts the head on he feels transformed: he entertains the company with brayings and kickings and, in Bottom's voice, orders sacks of oats and a bottle of hay. With some difficulty Shakespeare begins the rehearsal which stops and starts as new ideas and lines of dialogue are suggested. Very soon the comedy springs to life.

———●———

How comes this gentle concord in the world

IV i second section: from *Enter Theseus, Hippolyta, Egeus* (l. 102) to end, and IV ii

THESEUS · HIPPOLYTA · EGEUS · HELENA ·
HERMIA · LYSANDER · DEMETRIUS · BOTTOM · QUINCE ·
FLUTE · SNOUT · STARVELING · SNUG

———●———

CONVERSATIONS FOR TWO

● 'Go, one of you; find out the forester.' An attendant hurries off to give Theseus' orders to his forester who is in charge of the hounds. But he is eager to tell him other news: how he found two couples asleep in the wood, including Egeus' missing daughter. He decided not to wake them and not to go back and tell his master. The old forester hopes this won't affect the hunt, for the hounds are eager for the chase.

● Egeus returns home to give his wife the good news that their daughter Hermia has been found. Demetrius wants to marry Helena now, and if he's that changeable perhaps it's better for Hermia to marry Lysander after all. Anyway, the Duke has persuaded him to allow the marriage.

● Puck watches the discovery of the lovers and hears Theseus rule that the couples shall marry. Now all is well again. All they remember seems a dream. Bottom, too, is back with his fellow craftsmen. Puck reports all this to Oberon, or tries to, because Oberon is busy with plans for a visit to India with Titania.

● 'And by the way let's recount our dreams.' The adventures of each character can be told and discussed with any of the other characters or with all of them in turn. For example, Demetrius might talk to Lysander first, recalling his dream, then to Hermia and Helena. They are, of course, amazed how the dreams match up and how real the events seemed at the time. Now they are happily in love and any disagreements or unhappiness in the past do not matter.

FREEZING THE MOMENT

A practical study of Act Four

In this short Act, the shortest in the play, the stories of the lovers and the fairies are brought to a happy resolution after the confusions of Act Three. With the coming of dawn the night of enchantment ends, the lovers leave the forest and Bottom makes his triumphant return to his fellow craftsmen.

This Act is divided into short units for practical work by four separate groups of six or more members. Group One's work starts with the opening of Scene 1 in this Act; the work of the other groups follows in the same order as the text of the play, ending with Bottom's exit with his fellows.

Each group's work contains four 'frames' or frozen moments when the action is stopped for a count of five and then resumed. An entrance, mime or speech may lead up to one of these frames which may be rehearsed and 'reshot' until the particular effect is achieved. It would be interesting to photograph these frames so that the work could be studied and compared. A display of the photographs with passages of text and comments by the group could be the basis of a class discussion on Shakespeare's dramatic techniques.

The essential aim of this work is simply to provide a series of goals for each group's work rather than running through a scene of the play. Each frame can be discussed and experimented with; and the particular entrance or exit, grouping or individual moment, or contrasting changes of pace and mood, can be seen and appreciated.

Group One: OBERON, TITANIA, PUCK, BOTTOM, two or more Fairies

Group Two: THESEUS, EGEUS, DEMETRIUS, LYSANDER, HELENA, HERMIA
Hippolyta and Attendants may be cast if players are available.

Group Three: THESEUS, HELENA, LYSANDER, HERMIA HIPPOLYTA, DEMETRIUS
Egeus and Attendants can also be cast.

Group Four: BOTTOM, QUINCE, FLUTE, SNOUT, STARVELING, SNUG

Group One
OBERON · TITANIA · PUCK · BOTTOM
two or more Fairies

1   *Entrance.* All the characters enter except Puck. Try out various ways of making this entrance. Do they all enter from the same place? Who enters first? Must Oberon be the last to enter? Do we hear them before they appear?

2 *Mime.* Work on the opening of the scene: sitting, Titania's love for her 'gentle joy', Bottom's orders, the fairies bowing, scratching and fetching things. Let the Fairies attend on Bottom quite seriously in one rehearsal; in another mock him and perhaps their mistress as well.

3 *Speech.* The first 'frame' or snapshot follows the two speeches below. After Bottom's words all the players freeze for a count of five. Oberon counts aloud, signalling the start and finish of the count with a magic sign. The action resumes after the count.

MUSTARDSEED What's your will?

BOTTOM Nothing, good Monsieur, but to help Cavalery Cobweb to scratch.

Frame One

The emphasis in this frame is the grouping of the players around Bottom. Their gestures of serving, bowing, scratching and, in Titania's case, of love, can all be seen.

4 *Mime.* In mime, Titania suggests music and Bottom asks for the tongs and the bones. Titania quickly offers some food; Bottom calls for 'good hay, sweet hay'. This mime should build up to broad comedy with Bottom's neighing, Titania's petting, and the Fairies' reactions.

5 *Speech.* The second frame follows the speeches below. The stage picture changes with the exit of the Fairies as Bottom sleeps, and the entrance of Puck. The pace slackens and the mood changes from comedy to a moment's stillness before Oberon's dramatic speech to 'good Robin'.

BOTTOM I have an exposition of sleep come upon me.

TITANIA Sleep thou, and I will wind thee in my arms. Fairies be gone, and be all ways away. *Exeunt Fairies* O, how I love thee! How I dote on thee! *They sleep. Enter Puck.*

OBERON Welcome, good Robin. Seest thou this sweet sight?

Frame Two

This frame marks the contrast between the standing, observing figures of Oberon and Puck and the sleeping figures. It also contrasts with the activity of the players in the first frame. Oberon makes his magic sign and begins the count after his speech to Puck.

6 *Mime*. Oberon releases Titania from his spell. She is delighted to see Oberon.

7 *Speech*. The third frame follows the speeches below. The grouping changes as Titania rises to her feet.

> TITANIA My Oberon, what visions have I seen! Methought
>   I was enamoured of an ass.
> OBERON There lies your love.
> TITANIA How came these things to pass?
>   O, how mine eyes do loathe his visage now!

Frame Three

This frame concentrates on Titania's loathing as she turns and looks at the monster she loved. Her expression changes quickly from her happy greeting to Oberon to one of shock and disgust. Oberon gives the count as before.

8 *Mime*. On Oberon's orders, Puck removes the ass's head from Bottom, and mimes his release from the spell. Oberon calls for music, takes Titania's hands and leads her into a dance.

9 *Speech*. The last frame follows Puck's speech. The dance stops abruptly. The night has ended. They listen to the morning lark 'in silence sad'.

> PUCK Fairy king, attend, and mark:
>   I do hear the morning lark.

Frame Four

This frame tries to capture the moment between night and day, the passing of the fairy world and the coming of the mortals'; it is a moment of stillness, beauty and sadness. Lying on the ground behind them, almost forgotten, is a reminder of the mortals' world, the still sleeping Bottom.

10 *Exit*. Oberon and Titania leave hand-in-hand, followed by Puck.

Group Two

THESEUS · EGEUS · DEMETRIUS · LY ANDER · HELENA
HERMIA

Hippolyta and any number of Attendants may be cast if
players are available, but they are not essential.

1   *Entrance*. Demetrius and Helena, Lysander and Hermia
are lying asleep as hunting horns sound off-stage. Theseus
and Egeus come in. If cast, Hippolyta will enter with
Theseus, followed by any Attendants. Their entrance is
lively and excited.

2   *Mime*. Theseus discovers the sleepers.

3   *Speech*. The first 'frame' or snapshot follows the speeches
below. After Egeus' words all the players freeze for a
count of five given by Theseus. The action resumes after
the count.

THESEUS But soft, what nymphs are these?

EGEUS   My lord, this is my daughter here asleep,
And this Lysander; this Demetrius is,
This Helena—old Nedar's Helena.
I wonder at their being here together.

Frame One

This frame shows the grouping of Theseus and others
around the sleepers. It contrasts Egeus' surprised and
frowning reaction with Theseus' understanding smiles.
Any Attendants can show varying degrees of curiousity,
wonder or amusement and knowing winks.

4   *Mime*. Theseus orders the huntsmen to wake the
sleepers. If no huntsmen/attendants have been cast,
Egeus can snatch up a horn and sound it himself very
close to the sleepers. Theseus and Hippolyta watch their
sudden, startled awakening with amusement.

5   *Speech*. The second frame follows Theseus's speech.

THESEUS Good morrow, friends—Saint Valentine is past!

Frame Two

This frame captures a moment of comedy as the lovers
are startled awake. The confusions of the night still fill

their minds. Now it is daylight and Theseus and his court stand before them. Try to obtain four different reactions from the lovers, experimenting with facial expression and small gestures.

6   *Mime.* The lovers struggle to their feet and try to explain how they came to be there. Lysander's muddled explanation draws smiles from Theseus and angry frowns from Egeus.

7   *Speech.* The third frame follows Egeus' speech which breaks upon the sleepy happiness of the lovers like a freak summer storm.

> EGEUS   Enough, enough—my lord, you have enough!
> I beg the law, the law upon his head.
> They would have stolen away, they would, Demetrius,
> Thereby to have defeated you and me

Frame Three

This frame concentrates on a moment of anger. We are reminded in a flash of the dispute in the opening scene of the play. The happiness of the lovers is still threatened. We see their alarm as Egeus speaks and they are abruptly thrust back into their own world.

8   *Mime.* Demetrius leads Helena forward by the hand to show his restored love for her. He joins the hands of Lysander and Hermia to show their love. Theseus watches and then nods his approval. He takes Egeus aside; he indicates his wish to see the lovers married; and the matter is settled.

9   *Speech.* The last frame follows Theseus' speech and exit.

> THESEUS   Away with us to Athens. Three and three,
> We'll hold a feast in great solemnity.
> *Theseus and Egeus, and any Attendants, exit.*

Frame Four

This frame holds a moment of amazed happiness. They are to be married! Now the events of the night seem even more remote and strange. Here, surely, is the real world, their world—but there was, wasn't there, another world, fantastic and magical? It is a moment when 'everything seems double'.

Group Three

THESEUS · HIPPOLYTA · DEMETRIUS · LYSANDER ·
HELENA · HERMIA

Egeus and Attendants can also be cast.

1   *Speech.* The first 'frame' or snapshot follows Theseus's speech below. Lysander and Hermia, Demetrius and Helena stand hand-in-hand before Theseus and Hippolyta. Egeus and the Attendants, if cast, are grouped around them.

> THESEUS These couples shall eternally be knit.
>   Away with us to Athens. Three and three,
>   We'll hold a feast in great solemnity.
>   Come, Hippolyta.
>
> *Theseus and Hippolyta begin to make their exit.*

Frame One

As Theseus counts aloud to five, all the players (including Theseus) freeze. This frame looks at the moment of exit and the relationship between the two groups. The lovers are watching the exit, but their eyes of full of unexpected joy. Theseus' words seem too good to be true; and they are dumbfounded.

2   *Mime.* The action resumes: Theseus and Hippolyta complete their exit. The lovers turn to their partners, holding out their hands to one another in happiness. The magical impossibility of the moment and of the night leaves them standing full of wonder.

3   *Speech.* The second frame follows the two speeches below. Theseus, now off-stage, gives the count of five.

> HERMIA Methinks I see these things with parted eye,
>   When everything seems double.
> HELENA So methinks,
>   And I have found Demetrius, like a jewel,
>   Mine own and not mine own.

Frame Two

This frame closes in on the amazed happiness of the two pairs of lovers. They stand, holding hands, smiling at one another. The world about them seems real, this lover each holds by the hands seems real—but last night, when there was pain and quarrels and hate: was that real and true? Their faces reflect this bewilderment as well as their love.

4 *Mime*. Suddenly Lysander drops Hermia's hands and walks quickly away. Hermia and the others stare at this cold rejection. Then Lysander turns, laughing, and throws out his arms to receive Hermia. Delighted, they see that Lysander has played out Hermia's words: 'When everything seems double'.

Now Demetrius repeats, amid laughter, the mime of rejecting and accepting Helena. Because Helena knows what is happening, she is able to play up to Demetrius' rejection by over-reacting with huge sighs and sobs.

5 *Speech*. The third frame follows the next two speeches.

DEMETRIUS Are you sure
That we are awake? It seems to me
That yet we sleep, we dream. Do not you think
The Duke was here, and bid us follow him?
HERMIA Yea, and my father.

Frame Three

This frame looks at the moment when reality is restored. With Hermia's mock-sour expression and her mention of her father they all know that the dream, whatever it was, is over. This is the real world—and they are to be married! Now their delight knows no bounds.

6 *Mime*. Lysander comically exaggerates Egeus' pompous walk and his finger-wagging rage. He mimes his words to Theseus:

Enough, enough—my lord, you have enough!
I beg the law, the law upon his head.
They would have stolen away, they would, Demetrius,
Thereby to have defeated you and me—

The others, especially Hermia, laugh and applaud. These reactions can be real or mimed.

7 *Speech*. The last frame follows the next two speeches. Lysander drops his role as Egeus to speak.

LYSANDER And he did bid us follow to the temple.

DEMETRIUS Why, then, we are awake. Let's follow him,
And by the way let's recount our dreams.

Frame Four

This frame reminds us of the frozen exit of Theseus in frame one. It holds the moment when the lovers are free to leave the confusions of the wood to return to their own world. Like Theseus, their frozen exit is full of joy. Hand-in-hand, leaping and laughing, we see in the five-count, the certainty of their love in the real world.

8 *Exit*. They complete their exit. Unobserved all this time is Bottom, who, as the lovers exit, begins to stir.

Group Four

BOTTOM · QUINCE · FLUTE · SNOUT · STARVELING SNUG.

1 *Speech*. The first 'frame' or snapshot follows Bottom's speech below. After Bottom's words he freezes for a count of five given by Quince who is off-stage at this moment. The action resumes after the count.

Bottom stirs and wakes.

BOTTOM When my cue comes, call me, and I will answer.
My next is 'Most fair Pyramus'. Heigh ho! Peter Quince! Flute the bellows-mender! Snout the tinker! Starveling! God's my life—stolen hence and left me asleep!—

Frame One

This frame focuses on the moment of Bottom's return to the reality of his own world. Only a disturbing memory of 'a most rare vision' remains. What matters to Bottom now is that he has been deserted by his fellows.

2 *Mime*. Bottom mimes his faint recollections of his

dream: what he thought he was, what he thought he had growing from his head. He dismisses these thoughts as too fantastic and, turning to visions of his performance before the Duke, hurries off to join the craftsmen.

3   *Entrance*. The craftsmen's entrance is mimed to suggest that they are still searching for Bottom and have now met together to report to Quince. They are worried and dejected: there is no hope for their play without him.

4   *Speech*. The second frame follows the next two speeches. The stage picture changes as the craftsmen turn and perhaps rise as Snug enters with news. But there is no news of Bottom—only a fresh turn of the knife to add to their misery. The count of five is given by Bottom.

> SNUG   Masters, the Duke is coming from the temple, and there is two or three lords and ladies more married. If our sport had gone forward, we had all been made men.
>
> FLUTE   O, sweet Bully Bottom! Thus hath he lost sixpence a day during his life.

Frame Two

This frame takes in the whole group of players at a moment of brief hope as Snug enters, swiftly followed a real sense of lost opportunity both for them and Bottom. It is a moment that sharpens the contrast with the joy that greets Bottom's return.

5   *Speech*. The third frame follows the next three speeches. Quince gives the count of five. There is a dejected pause as the craftsmen take in Snug's news. Flute continues his requiem for Bottom.

> FLUTE   An the Duke had not given him sixpence a day for playing Pyramus, I'll be hanged. (*Snug sniffs softly.*) He would have deserved it. (*Much sad nodding of heads and sympathetic looks.*) Sixpence a day in Pyramus, or nothing. (*True, o true: they bow their heads.*)
>
> *Enter Bottom behind them; a pause, then—*
>
> BOTTOM   Where are these lads? Where are these hearts?
>
> QUINCE   Bottom!

Frame Three

This frame holds the moment of Bottom's stunning entrance. There is joy, astonishment, relief, noise and movement. The mood of the scene is transformed by this resurrection. It is, as Bottom knows, a tremendous moment, a really successful performance.

6   *Mime.* Experiment with reactions to Bottom's entrance. Are the craftsmen so stunned by Bottom's return that they sit and stare at him in disbelief? Quince, by his words, is clearly the first to rise and welcome Bottom. The others, perhaps, come forward more cautiously as if they feared some kind of witchcraft.

Then it is all cheers and greetings and handshakings and back-slapping until Bottom silences them. They must prepare the play: collect their costumes, dress and make-up, make sure of their lines. O, they are ready, they are eager! Their confidence soars as Bottom's breezy authority sweeps over them.

7   *Speech.* The last frame follows Bottom's speech. Quince gives the count.

> BOTTOM   And, most dear actors, eat no onions nor garlic; for we are to utter sweet breath, and I do not doubt but to hear them say it is a sweet comedy.

Frame Four

This frame is concerned with the emotions of the whole group around Bottom. In contrast with the second frame, Snug's entrance, they are now alert and excited. They guffaw with delight at Bottom's apt joke and cheer his declaration that their audience will say 'it is a sweet comedy'.

8   *Exit.* There is work to do. Bottom is back and all's well. They make a happy, eager exit.

TALKING ABOUT ACTING 13

———————— ● ————————

PETER BROOK rehearsing his production of the play

The quartet of sleeping lovers lolled perilously upon swings suspended from the flies: Bottom lay motionless below seeming dead to the world. On another side of the stage, Oberon was waiting to catch a spinning plate on a pole tossed down by Puck from a high balcony. He missed, shrugged ('Take 342!') and tried again. In the front stalls of the Stratford auditorium Peter Brook was watching the fraught rehearsal of *A Midsummer Night's Dream* calmly and without any visible signs of anxiety or doubt.

He is directing the *Dream* unaided by the obvious pretty-pretty fairy enchantments. Props and movements have been shaped from a circus ring rather than a haunted wood. He doesn't worry when things go wrong—the actors must make their own magic. During the second week of rehearsals, when the text had yet to be opened, the actors had improvised a happening around the theme of the *Dream*. 'It had extraordinary force and interest,' states Brook. 'But like all happenings it can never be repeated— it was there once and gone.' Far from neglecting the text of the play, Brook's involvement in a work which interests him is total. For this Shakespeare comedy, his actors must never be allowed to forget that they are playing in the context of continual stage happenings, a world 'swift as a shadow, short as any dream.'

'After a series of dark, violent, black plays I had a very strong wish to go as deeply as possible into a work of pure celebration. *A Midsummer Night's Dream* is, amongst other things, a celebration of the arts of the theatre. One one level the actors have to display a physical virtuosity—an expression of joy. Hence our production at Stratford involves acrobatics, circus skills, trapeze acts. Equally, certain parts of the play cannot be played without using a Stanislavkian sense of natural character development. There's the play we all know—and also a hidden play, a hidden dream. That's the one the actors set out to discover for themselves.

'The *Dream* is a play about magic, spirits, fairies. Today we don't believe in any one of those things and yet, perhaps we do.

The fairy imagery which the Victorian tradition has given us has to be rejected—it has died on us. But one can't take an anti-magical, a down-to-earth view of the *Dream*. The interest in working on the *Dream* is to take a play which is apparently composed of very artificial, unreal elements and to discover that it is a true, a real play. But the language of the *Dream* must be expressed through a very different stage imagery from the one which served its purpose in the past.

'We have dropped all pretence of making magic by bluff, through stage tricks. The first step must be moving from darkness to daylight. We have to start in the open—in fact we begin with a white set and white light (the only darkness in the entire production occurs during the public encounters between Theseus and Hippolyta). We present all the elements with which we are going to work in the open. This is related to one of the key lines in the play when the question arises about whether the man who is going to play the lion should be a real lion or only pretend to be real. Out of this comes the formulation that the actor should say to the audience, "I am a man as other men are". That is the necessary beginning for a play about the spirit world—the actors must present themselves as men who are like all other men. It's from the hidden inner life of the performer that the magic, the unfolding possibilities of the play, must emerge.

'The core of the *Dream* is the Pyramus and Thysbe play which doesn't come at the end of a highly organised work just for comic relief. The actor's art is truly celebrated in this episode—it becomes a mysterious interplay of invisible elements, the joy, the magic of the *Dream*. The play can become an exploration, through a complex series of themes, of what only the theatre can do as an art form.'

PETER BROOK talking to Peter Ansorge;
Plays and Players, October 1970

Imaginative written work

● A Missing Scene of Oberon's meeting with Titania and Bottom is described on page 105. Write a group play, *A*

Most Rare Vision after improvising it.
● Describe a rehearsal of the Bottom-Titania scene at the Globe, which is suggested on page 107. Bring some details of the theatre into your account.
● Watch, or take part in, any one of the four stage rehearsals of Act IV which are described on pages 109–119. Keep a Rehearsal Diary recording the players' progress and how the various problems are overcome, or write a play review of the performance or final rehearsal.
● Bottom thinks he will ask Peter Quince to write a ballad of his dream, to be called *Bottom's Dream*. As Peter Quince, kindly supply the ballad, or if you prefer, a story or a diary.
● Write a newspaper report on the strange disappearance of Bottom and provide a follow-up story of his equally inexplicable reappearance. Your articles can include interviews with the principals.
● As a fashion writer, describe the three weddings of Theseus and the two pairs of lovers. You may write as an Elizabethan or from a modern point of view. You may include various items of gossip and interviews with the brides.
● An open discussion on Peter Brook's ideas about his production of this play, reported in Talking About Acting 13. A group might rehearse this discussion privately and then, using a chairman to offer leading questions, repeat it in public.

ACT FIVE
Imagination

STARVELING . . . *All that I have to say is to tell you that the lantern is the moon, I the man i'th'moon, this thorn bush my thorn bush, and this dog my dog.*

———————●———————

ACT FIVE
Scene I

It must be your imagination, then, and not theirs.

V i first section: from *Enter Theseus, Hippolyta, Philostrate*
to *Exeunt Theseus, Hippolyta* (l. 360)

THESEUS · HIPPOLYTA · PHILOSTRATE · HELENA ·

HERMIA · DEMETRIUS · LYSANDER · BOTTOM · QUINCE · FLUTE ·

SNUG · STARVELING · SNOUT · ATTENDANTS

———————⬤———————

CONVERSATIONS FOR TWO

● Egeus is not present at the celebrations for the Duke's marriage. Egeus is unwilling to allow his daughter to marry Lysander; he feels Demetrius is a far better match. The Duke points out that Demetrius now loves Helena; he must let true love take its own course. Egeus still feels that his authority has been flouted. He quarrels with the Duke, who says the marriage will go forward as he decides. And Egeus refuses to attend the wedding.

● Philostrate is afraid that the craftsmen's play will displease the Duke and decides to cancel their performance and alter the programme before the Duke sees it. He tries to explain this to Bottom.

● Flute is dressing for his part as Thisbe. He feels embarrassed and alarmed at the sight of so many lords and ladies. Helena sees and understands his misery. She knows what it's like to be laughed at (she speaks these thoughts aloud). She gives him confidence by talking to him as if she thought he really was a woman.

●   Where I have come, great clerks have purposèd
        To greet me with premeditated welcomes

As Theseus leaves the church after his marriage to

Hippolyta, he is officially invited to attend the city's festivities in his honour. The official is very nervous and hesitant, frequently breaking off in the middle of a sentence, and forgetting his main points. Theseus treats him kindly and praises his good intentions.

● After their performance of the play, Bottom and Flute talk it over. They are both delighted with the success of their own performances and with the audience's applause for the whole play. Bottom can't help comparing his efforts with those of Starveling as Moon and Snout as Wall; and surely the audience shouldn't have laughed so much? Flute is certain that were he a younger man he might have become an excellent actor.

●   And all their minds transfigured so together
    . . . grows to something of great constancy . . .

Hippolyta feels she can understand what the lovers have experienced in their combined dream, but to Theseus these events, seen in the light of cool reason are 'more strange than true.' He feels that if the events happened at all they are simply a set of mechanical misunderstandings. She compares their present complete happiness with their various troubles only a day before.

● Two Elizabethan housewives (possibly wives of players), watch the craftsmen's play. To them it is a fine tragedy and they enjoy crying over the sad death of the lovers. Their imaginative involvement is so great that they see no fault in the playing and cannot understand the laughter of the court; but perhaps there were jokes which they, simple folk, couldn't appreciate. Together with their delight in the play, they mix shrewd comments on the weddings and the brides' dresses.

TALKING ABOUT ACTING 14

━━━ ● ━━━

The Pyramus and Thisbe Interlude

His first entrance as Pyramus, superbly arrogant, drinking down every smatter of applause with thirsty relish, his tussles with the Davy Crocket fur tail on his helmet that always seemed to be in his mouth, his battles with the recalcitrant Thisbe, his contempt for Peter Quince who forgot to stain the mantle with lion's blood, his pained reception of the interruptions from various spectators—all this built up into clowning of the most inspired, irresistible kind. Moreover he was aided, abetted and sometimes equalled by the quavery Moonshine, clutching lanthorn, dog and bush of thorns in only two hands and then trying to mount a footstool despite the impediments of a long white nightgown, the faithful Wall, who was quite intimidated by Pyramus' rages, and the feckless Thisbe who, in an endeavour to simulate grief, tore out one of her flaxen plaits by the very roots.

MARY CLARKE reviewing Michael Bentall's 1957 production at the Old Vic; *Shakespeare at the Old Vic 5* Hamish Hamilton

━━━ ● ━━━

PAIR WORK

Pyramus and Thisbe
FIRST PAIR
Peter Quince's first speech:

> If we offend it is with our good will.

This text, and the others below, can be read in rehearsal, or learnt or closely improvised.

Working method
The aim is to play the reading of this speech in character, addressing it to your partner who represents a V.I.P. like Theseus. First rehearsals can be played sitting down, but later Quince should act on his feet, coming forward to speak to Theseus who remains seated.

Experiments

Experiment freely with voice, movement and mannerisms. Discuss how you see this character and how this speech would be read on such an occasion. Try different accents and ages for the voice, varying lengths of hesitation, various signs of nervousness. Your final aim is to work out a detailed performance between you.

SECOND PAIR

Snout as Wall, speech beginning:

> In this same interlude it doth befall

Use the working method described above.

The aim is to show how Snout is always Snout, and is never absorbed in his part. For movement, the player needs to remember that he may be wearing material to represent the wall, and might be inside a wooden framework with only hands and face fully visible.

Experiment as above, with voice, movement and mannerisms. Try to achieve Snout's slow, heavy-handed explanation and native simplicity. Discuss the success of each experiment.

THIRD PAIR

Bottom as Pyramus. His first speech:

> O grim-looked night, O night with hue so black,

Bottom has so much boisterous energy that his part should be played on the feet from the start of rehearsals.

Working on voice, the player can experiment with the many O's, his glances at the audience for their approval (represented by the partner), and his tremendous enjoyment in acting or over-acting. Like Snout he is never in his part, but he is far from being nervous.

Working on movement, the player must be conscious of wall which can be marked by chairs or played by the partner. He also directs everything very forcibly at his audience like a villain in a melodrama.

FOURTH PAIR
Flute as Thisbe, Bottom as Pyramus
from FLUTE O wall, full often hast thou heard my moans
to FLUTE Tide life, tide death, I come without delay.

This involves both players working on the text at the same time. See the notes on Bottom, above. If played by a boy, Flute must be aware that he is wearing a long dress, but remains a working man playing a sophisticated lady in love without any conviction at all. If the part is played by a girl, she must attempt to portray the heavy manliness of the part. Movement is particularly important here.

FIFTH PAIR
Snug as Lion, speech beginning:

   You, ladies—you whose gentle hearts do fear

Here the movement and the roaring are important. We are always aware that Snug is playing the lion, and playing so that no one will think he is real. Lion-like movements can be interrupted by human gestures; a cloth or papier-maché mask will help with the business. Like the others, Snug is not conscious of any humour in his part or in his playing.

SIXTH PAIR
Starveling as Moonshine
from STARVELING This lanthorn doth the horned moon present
to DEMETRIUS Why, all these should be in the lantern; for all these are in the moon. But silence: here comes Thisbe.

Partner can speak the various speeches between Starveling's lines. Starveling may be irritated by these interruptions and embarrassed by the comments; he may be pleased to be the subject of so much attention; he may wait out of respect until the lords have finished speaking; he may simply forget what to say next. Experiment with these possibilities, combining several for the final performance. Simple properties will help with the business.

SEVENTH PAIR
Bottom as Pyramus, Starveling as Moonshine
from BOTTOM O wherefore, nature, didst thou lions frame,
to He dies

Bottom now reaches the climax of his part, which he delivers with tremendous gusto and tragic fire. For comic effect—though not to Bottom—his sword may stick in the scabbard, or be too short or too long; and his death may be a very lengthy business with a series of recoveries for the next word (die . . . die . . . die) or the the next line, as after Moonshine's exit.

Moonshine's reactions will greatly add to the comic effect. He may be entranced by Bottom's performance; he may register alarm and horror at his death so that 'Moon, take thy flight' acts as a necessary reminder of his part. He may also pursue Bottom about the stage, shedding his Moonshine on the action but annoying Bottom by getting in his way and detracting from his great performance.

EIGHTH PAIR
Flute as Thisbe
from FLUTE Asleep, my love?
to She dies

Partner can play the dead Pyramus. The notes on Thisbe for the Fourth Pair apply here. Flute may have the same trouble with the sword as Bottom; and it may, for example, be tightly trapped under Bottom's body and so require considerable strength to extricate it.

THE ARTIST'S POINT OF VIEW
Comedy or tragedy?

> . . . All for your delight
> We are not here.

The workers' production of *Pyramus and Thisbe* is designed for laughter. This is the artist's point of view; the workers, of course, aim at tragedy, but their efforts are deliberately frustrated by the language and the punctuation of the play and by their inability to lose themselves in their parts.

The comic effect of the play is also achieved by the outside and detached view of the lovers in the play. Like Theseus and his friends we are observers who are never drawn into the life of the action and the characters; we are never moved by their love or death.

While writing *A Midsummer Night's Dream* and *Romeo and Juliet* Shakespeare saw that the same plot (for *Pyramus and Thisbe*) and the theme of love could be treated as either tragic or comic. Broadly, while comedy could be achieved by a detached view of character and action, tragedy required insight: a point of view from within, from Romeo's or Juliet's point of view. So we see the world with their eyes and love and suffer with them.

PERFORMANCE

These two points of view can be played and compared in discussion. The extracts from *Romeo and Juliet* and the *Pyramus and Thisbe* Interlude can be read by four players without any attempt to act in terms of movement. Discuss the speeches as examples of dramatic writing: parody and poetic drama. Then learn or closely improvise the speeches and discuss the effect of each kind of writing in performance.

JULIET   Come, night. Come, Romeo. Come, thou day in night;
For thou wilt lie upon the wings of night
Whiter than new snow on a raven's back.
Come, gentle night. Come, loving, black-browed night.
Give me my Romeo.

(III ii, lines 17 to 21)

PYRAMUS   O grim-looked night, O night with hue so black,
O night which ever art when day is not!
O night, O night, alack, alack, alack,
I fear my Thisbe's promise is forgot.

ROMEO   Eyes, look your last!
Arms, take your last embrace! and, lips, O you
The doors of breath, seal with a righteous kiss
A dateless bargain to engrossing death!
Come, bitter conduct, come, unsavoury guide!
Thou desperate pilot, now at once run on
The dashing rocks thy seasick weary bark!
Here's to my love! (*He drinks*) O true apothecary!
Thy drugs are quick. Thus with a kiss I die.

                               (V iii, 112 to 120)

PYRAMUS Eyes, do you see?—
How can it be?
O dainty duck, O dear!
Thy mantle good—
What, stained with blood!
Approach, ye Furies fell.

. . . .

Come tears, confound;
Out sword, and wound
The pap of Pyramus.
Ay, that left pap,
Where heart doth hop.
Thus die I—thus, thus, thus.
                He stabs himself.
Now am I dead,
Now am I fled;
My soul is in the sky.
Tongue, lose thy light;
            Exit Starveling as Moonshine.
Moon, take thy flight;
Now die, die, die, die, die.   *He dies.*

(Juliet wakes from her drugged sleep in the tomb. Friar
Lawrence tells her that Romeo is dead. He will take her
to a nunnery before the Watch comes.)

JULIET   Go, get thee hence, for I will not away.
What's here? A cup, closed in my true love's hand?
Poison, I see, hath been his timeless end.
O churl! drunk all, and left no friendly drop

	To help me after? I will kiss thy lips.
	Haply some poison yet doth hang on them
	To make me die with a restorative. *She kisses him*
	Thy lips are warm!
WATCH	Lead, boy. Which way?
JULIET	Yea, noise? Then I'll be brief. O happy dagger!
	This is thy sheath; there rust, and let me die.
	She stabs herself and falls
THISBE	Asleep, my love?
	What, dead, my dove?
	O Pyramus, arise.
	Speak, speak. Quite dumb?
	Dead, dead? A tomb
	Must cover thy sweet eyes.
	These lily lips,
	This cherry nose,
	These yellow cowslip cheeks
	Are gone, are gone.
	Lovers, make moan—
	His eyes were green as leeks.
	. . . .
	Come, trusty sword,
	Come blade, my breast imbrue. *She stabs herself*
	And farewell friends.
	Thus Thisbe ends.
	Adieu, adieu, adieu! *She dies*

———————•———————

From the presence of the sun
Following darkness like a dream,
Now are frolic.

V i second section: from *Exeunt Theseus, Hippolyta* . . . (l. 360)
to end
OBERON · TITANIA · PUCK · FAIRIES

————————•————————

CONVERSATIONS FOR TWO

● In old age, Bottom and Quince recall the great occasion of their performance before the lords and ladies. Bottom seems able to remember every detail clearly, though sometimes his version conflicts with what Quince remembers.

● Many years later Theseus and Hippolyta sit dreaming of times past: how the families of the lovers have grown up, how they laughed at the craftsmen's play, and how they never really understood, or believed, the strange tales told by the lovers about their night in the wood.

● Some years later Oberon and Titania return to the wood which stirs up memories of their quarrel over the changeling child. Titania remembers everything perfectly, but Oberon seems to have forgotten all about it, and he is not anxious to call Puck as a witness. That particular night, he suggests, was so full of magic and love that she is confused; after all, it all ended happily.

● Two Elizabethan women leave the Globe after a performance of this play. This last fairy scene reminds the first of a similar house which seemed blessed, and reminds the second of a house which seemed cursed. Each is anxious to tell her own story and to convince the other; neither is willing to listen; but they agree that 'strange things do happen'.

ENDING THE PLAY

Dream or reality?

> The iron tongue of midnight hath told twelve.
> Lovers, to bed; 'tis almost fairy time.

It would have been a simple plan to keep the fairy world to the centre of the play and to end as it began with the world of the mortals. Then the fairy world would be seen as a dream by the mortals: it didn't really happen, it was just a dream, nothing more. But Shakespeare's dream world invades reality: mortals and fairies are all shadows, and only our imagination gives them reality. So the play ends with a blessing from one world upon the other.

PERFORMANCE
As the play of Pyramus and Thisbe proceeds and the day passes, so the mood changes from comedy to midnight music and dance and fairy blessing. The turning point is strongly marked by the exit of the craftsmen and of Theseus: the stage empties. The story is over. A pause, a silence; and Puck· runs in alone. The stage fills again; until, alone again, Puck bids the audience good-night. The changing stage picture draws us from one world to another, while each reminds us of the other.

GROUP PLAYS

If we offend
Learn or improvise closely Quince's prologue beginning, 'If we offend it is with our good will', and Puck's final speech to the audience beginning, 'If we shadows have offended'. Speak these lines, using one player or two, at the start and at the finish of the following group plays.

● A short mime of the Pyramus and Thisbe play.
BOTTOM · FLUTE · STARVELING · SNUG · SNOUT · QUINCE · PUCK
● A dance-drama, with music, for the fairy blessing on the house and the three couples.
OBERON · TITANIA · QUINCE · PUCK · FAIRY ATTENDANTS.
● Combine the mimed play and the dance-drama, using Theseus' speech, 'The iron tongue of midnight hath told twelve' as a link, in addition to the two other speeches at the beginning and end.
● Choose *any* other scene, or part of one, and play in mime or as an improvisation. Use the two speeches for Quince and Puck as before.

● On stage with lighting effects and music. Combine the mimed play of Pyramus and Thisbe with a dance-drama for the fairy blessing. Use music throughout, except for the speeches of Quince and Puck. Gradually lower lighting, from day-light, during the mimed play; also reduce the fire-effect as the fire dies down; introduce moon-light effect to evoke fairy world atmosphere; end with solitary Spot on Puck at the end, with slow fade out.

● To the above, add choral speech and reduce the volume of music by holding it behind the speakers and only bringing it up as required.

Choral work

Quince's prologue; Quince's outline of the story, beginning 'Gentles, perchance you wonder at this show'; Theseus' speech, 'The iron tongue of midnight . . .'; Oberon's speech, 'Now until the break of day'; and Puck's 'Now the hungry lion roars'.

Solo speech

Oberon's speech, 'Through the house give glimmering light'; and Titania's following speech, 'First rehearse your song by rote'; finally Puck's last speech.

If lighting effects are not available, the choral work can simply be added to the mimed play and the dance-drama. For choral work the speeches can be read or learnt. Five groups could each work on one of the suggested choral speeches, with other groups preparing the mime and the dance. A small team of electricians can be appointed.

TALKING ABOUT ACTING 15

Above all it must be stressed that the production had been *fun*— a joyous celebration of the actors' skills in which the limitation of these in the classical field to intelligent vocal manipulation of the verse had been smashed through as only a *part* of a more acrobatic concept of the actor as a conjurer, a trapeze artist—a being with one foot in the circus and one on Shakespeare's text.

It was immensely cheering to see the final vestiges of the idea of a Shakespeare actor being essentially a rather dignified declamatory artist so boldly jettisoned whilst the verse itself remained unmutilated.

PETER ROBERTS reviewing Peter Brook's 1970 production
at Stratford-upon-Avon; *Plays and Players*, October 1970

Imaginative written work
● One of the Conversations on page 124 refers to an official welcome speech for Theseus. The city mayor offers congratulations on his marriage and invites him to attend the festivities arranged in his honour. Write the speech as the mayor prepared it, and then as he spoke it to Theseus.
● After working on the Pyramus and Thisbe play, look at the play review on page 126. Compare your group performance with this professional production, noting differences of interpretation, details of business and the style of playing: whether subtle, broad, gentle, coarse . . .
● Describe your rehearsal of any of the Pair work for Pyramus and Thisbe on pages 126–129. Note what points were easy or difficult, what kind of solutions you found, and how far the rehearsal contributed to your understanding of that speech or the scene in general.
● *The Artist's Point of View* is discussed on page 129. After a reading or performance of the extracts from *Romeo and Juliet* and *Pyramus and Thisbe*, describe how the artist's intention is achieved. It will be helpful if you have taken part in the reading or performance yourself.
● Write a play review of the craftsmen's play from the point of view of a sympathetic Elizabethan working man or woman.
● Write a play review of the craftsmen's play from the point of view of one of Theseus' guests at his wedding.
● As Bottom, write a review of *Pyramus and Thisbe*,

giving full praise where it is due. You can also comment on the reactions of the audience.

● As the actress playing both Juliet and Thisbe in the extracts, comment on the problems of each role, whether acted or read, and how you attempted to solve them. You can also say which you found easier, which more enjoyable.

● As an actor playing both Romeo and Pyramus in the extracts, comment on your role as above.

● As an Elizabethan producer of the Pyramus and Thisbe Interlude, describe the difficulties you had to face in terms of set, properties such as the stained mantle and the lanthorn, the dialogue and the abilities of the actors. In this the producer should be seen as actually producing this play with working men in real life, and not as part of Shakespeare's play.

● Write a commentary to be spoken during one of the Group Plays, *If We Offend*. It may be used in connection with the mime, the dance-drama, the stage performance (the fifth suggestion) or the choral performance. This should be written after watching or taking part in one of these.

● Puck speaks the epilogue to the audience at the end of the play. As Bottom, Helena or Theseus, write your own epilogue to complete a performance of this play. This can be in verse, free or rhymed, or in prose.

GROUP PROJECTS

These projects involve research into aspects of the play which can be undertaken by one group and then presented to the rest of the class in various ways, or the whole class sharing the work between them.

● *An exposition of sleep*
All the lovers and Titania and Bottom fall asleep during the play's action—some of them more than once. Look up all these occasions, mark out sufficient dialogue to explain how and why each falls asleep, provide a commentary

to link up the scenes and perform as an improvisation or
as a series of learnt extracts.

● *Spells and charms*

The fairies and Oberon and Puck frequently demonstrate
their magic powers during the play; Titania's fairies
weave a protective magic circle about their mistress while
Puck and Oberon use the juice of Cupid's flower. Look up
these occasions, mark out sufficient dialogue to explain
how and why each spell or charm is used, provide a
commentary to link up the scenes and perform as an
improvisation or learnt script.

● Using the material suggested above, prepare a mime or
dance-drama based on the theme of magic powers.
Either of these can be provided with a commentary or a
chorus which repeats some of the spells. The sequence
can end with the fairies' blessing on the three married
couples.

● *The inconstant moon*

The play deals largely with the events of a single night,
and the moon helps to create the fairy world, and the
mortals' world of strange dreams and romance. The word
'moon' occurs five times in the first scene alone. Collect
together references to the moon, including synonyms like
'Phoebe', and present your quotations as short readings
linked by a commentary.

● *Short as any dream*

The word 'dream' is a similar key-word to 'moon', above.
How this word is used can be examined by collecting the
references, arranging a reading with a prepared commentary and discussing the result with your audience.

● *Such tricks hath strong imagination*

How does Shakespeare create his fairy world? Select
information which you feel contributes to this and
arrange a series of readings. Against this present, either as
readings or as a play, a fairground—a bright and gaudy
world, but unlike the normal world—with its Tunnel of
Love, Distorting Mirrors, and Fortune-teller.

● *The form of things unknown*
Present a different, though known, world: a railway
station at night inhabited by reluctant travellers, a
Station Master and a Ticket Collector. 'Or in the night ...
how easy is a bush supposed a bear!' Mark the parallels
with Shakespeare's play by reading a number of short
extracts.
● Philostrate offers Theseus four choices for his entertainment. We see nothing of the other three. Write a script for
one of them and perform it in an appropriate style
before Theseus. The players need not, of course, be Bottom
and his friends.
● *But all the story of the night told over*
Regard the events of the palace and the wood as a series of
fascinating news stories for either a daily newspaper or a
radio broadcast. In addition to news you can present
interviews, gossip, speculation, discussion and comment.
Similarly, you could present a series of TV broadcasts;
this would enable you to interview 'live' and to give
some outside broadcasts with commentators describing
the scene on the spot.
● There is another play-within-a-play in *Love's Labour's
Lost*. The *Pageant of the Nine Worthies* is in V ii. Perform
this as a group play before the king and his court. In
discussion, this play can be compared with *Pyramus and
Thisbe* which could also be performed, either by the same
group or by another.

BOOK LIST

A comprehensive list of books would be virtually endless.
I have found the following stimulating and helpful.

BROWN, JOHN RUSSELL, *Shakespeare's Plays in Performance*,
Penguin Shakespeare Library, 1969.

BROWN, JOHN RUSSELL, *Shakespeare and his Comedies*,
Methuen, 1957.

HALLIDAY, F. E., *A Shakespeare Companion*, Penguin
Shakespeare Library, 1964. (Contains an excellent
bibliography on all aspects of Shakespeare and his
work).

KOTT, JAN, *Shakespeare Our Contemporary*, Methuen, 1964.

LERNER, LAURENCE, ed., *Shakespeare's Comedies, an anthology
of modern criticism* Penguin Shakespeare Library, 1967.

QUENNELL, PETER, *Shakespeare: the poet and his background*,
Penguin Shakespeare Library, 1969.

RIGHTER, ANNE, *Shakespeare and the Idea of the Play*, Penguin
Shakespeare Library, 1969.

TILLYARD, E. M. W., *The Elizabethan World Picture*, Chatto
& Windus, 1967.

WICKHAM, GLYNNE, *Shakespeare's Dramatic Heritage*,
Routledge & Kegan Paul, 1969.

WILLIAMS, C. J., *Theatres and Audiences*, Longman, 1970.

Stage craft

ADLAND, DAVID, *The Group Approach to Drama Book 4*
Longmans, 1967, (for a practical introduction to stage
craft and the construction of school stages and sets).

CHAMBERS, E. K., *The Elizabethan Stage*, Oxford University
Press, 1923.

HODGES, C. WALTER, *The Globe Restored*, Oxford University
Press, 1968.

STYAN, J. L., *Shakespeare's Stagecraft*, Cambridge University
Press, 1967.

Music
In addition to Benjamin Britten's A Midsummer Night's
Dream and a number of other well-known classical pieces,
there is a wide range of recorded Elizabethan music
available. The following list offers a selection (numbers
are for mono recordings).
Music of Shakespeare's Time CLP 1633 and CLP 1634.
Shakespeare's Songs and Lute Solos ALP 1265.
Music of Sixteenth Century England TFL 6022.
Church Music of Tallis and Weelkes RG 237.
Church Music of William Byrd RG 226.
Church Music of Orlando Gibbons RG 151.
English Music of the Early Seventeenth Century AXA
4515.
John Dowland: Songs and Ayres H 1167
Masque Music H 1153

ACKNOWLEDGEMENTS

We are grateful to the following for permission to reproduce copyright material:

Edward Arnold (Publishers) Ltd. for three extracts from *Shakespeare's Plays in Performance* by J. R. Brown; Plays and Players for an extract from Peter Brook talking to Peter Ansorage in 'Directors in Interview', *Plays and Players*, October 1970 and Peter Roberts for an extract from a review of 1970 Royal Shakespeare Company production of *Midsummer Night's Dream;* Cambridge University Press for two extracts from *Shakespeare Survey* by J. R. Brown; Hamish Hamilton Ltd., London, for four extracts from *Shakespeare at the Old Vic vol. 5* ed. Mary Clarke; the author for an extract from a review of the 1970 Royal Shakespeare Company production of Midsummer Night's Dream by Peter Roberts published in *Plays and Players;* The Sunday Times for three extracts from a review by Harold Hobson of A Midsummer Night's Dream, published in *The Sunday Times* of 13 June 1971.